ISBN-13: 978-1-950959-00-6

Tattoos

as

Punishment

An Illustrated History of Japanese Tattooing

BY ERIC SHAHAN

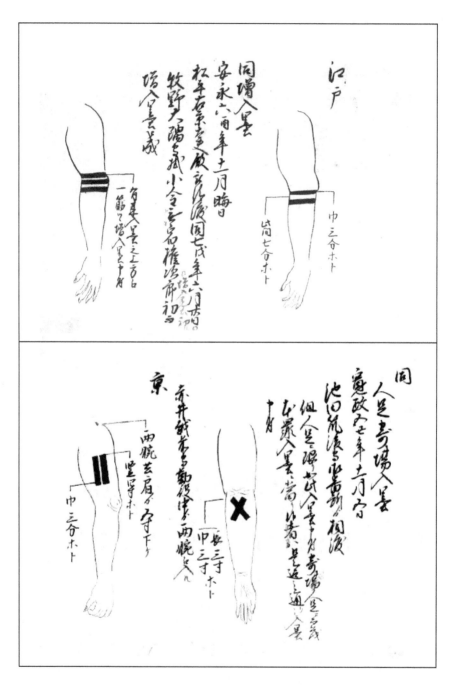

Manual describing how prisoners should be tattooed in Edo (top and bottom right) and Kyoto (bottom left.) 19th century

Introduction

I have translated over two dozen ancient Japanese books on Martial Arts, Philosophy and Ninjutsu (the art of the ninja) but this is the first book that I have written myself, so this is a new experience.

I did not start an expert on tattoos, but knew of a common belief that the practice of tattooing in Japan began with the use of punishment tattoos of convicted criminals by the authorities, a practice adopted from the Chinese legal system. The story goes that criminals with punishment tattoos began to add to them and a subculture that appreciated tattooing began to emerge. While initially part of the underworld, specifically the Yakuza, Japan's organized crime and gamblers, tattooing spread to and became more popular with other social groups. Or so the story supposedly goes.

But the more I read the more I found this belief was wildly inaccurate.

Overview

While my initial plan was to translate a few books and research papers from the Meiji era (1868-1911) through the early Showa era (1925-1940), but I found that books on tattooing were fairly scarce and tended to overlap. The same short passages on ancient Japanese tattooing and Ainu tattooing appeared in book after book and I began to believe that some of the published researchers didn't really want to find the true tattooing tradition of Japan. So instead of translating a series of short works from the early modern era of Japan, I began to research more deeply. As a result, this book is an overview of tattooing in Japan from ancient times up through the modern era.

Research Method

Modern technology has made researching much easier, but because this is Japanese everything is several orders of magnitude more difficult than in most modern languages. Written Japanese has changed dramatically over the pre-modern, early modern, and modern era, and most early materials cannot be recovered by Optical Character Reader software. Indeed, most educated Japanese today cannot read the ancient characters written in an array of styles, ranging from clearly legible block characters to obscure cursive styles that can defeat the most determined and experienced researcher. Digital catalogues and digital libraries at best can only provide what you ask for, and there are many different words used in the technical and descriptive vocabulary of tattooing in Japanese as shown on page 8. Eventually I had to search databases multiple times as I uncovered different terms that allowed me to retrieve more information. One very useful paper was Tanaka Kogai's 田中香涯 (1874-1944) *Tattooing,* part of a larger work titled *Medical Trivia: Unusual, Strange and Spooky* 醫事雜考:妖,異,變 published in 1941.

While brief, Tanaka attempted to cover Japanese tattooing from ancient times to the modern era and showed tattooing traditions outside the realm of punishment tattoos. This short paper gave me a lot of hints regarding where to look for more information, and I am grateful to him for this very useful introduction.

Organization and Sources

This book is organized chronologically; however, since tattooing in the Ainu culture of the northern islands and the Ryukyu (Okinawan) southern islands developed independently (probably) it is difficult to be truly chronological, so these were handled independently.

We are all very fortunate that early 20[th]century researchers such as Mitsuoka Shinichi and Tanaka Kogai were kind enough to comb through 17th century literature and discover references to tattooing in literature. Thanks to modem digital libraries I was able to find the books they referenced and include sections of them herein. Also, certain other researchers were kind enough to transcribe the difficult Edo era Japanese text into modern font Kanji. These transcriptions made it possible for me to translate sections of these heretofore illegible (for most non-specialists) texts for the first time. These Edo era examples of Japanese popular literature captured contemporary Japanese society. The books were popular with the emerging merchant class and no doubt with Samurai as well (albeit covertly due to the fact they were supposed to live austere lives.) The books consist of romance novels, woodblock print Manga stories and salacious compendiums of brothel rumors. Though these works we can catch a glimpse of how tattooing was perceived during the Edo Era 1604-1868.

The final sources are legal documents detailing how tattooing as punishment was conducted, including specific cases that resulted in conviction and a criminal being tattooed. These were also been transcribed from period legal documents and police records and detail the specific crimes that resulted in a specific punishment tattoo. These last sources are fascinating "true crime" stories that bring the history alive with detail. Their names, dates, crimes and subsequent punishments were recorded as "example cases" in order to be used by Edo Era police as a standard by which other criminals were judged, convicted and tattooed.

Acknowledgements

I would like to thank my mother, Linda Shahan, for all her help.

I also owe a large debt to my de-facto editor, Lance Gatling, without whom this work would not be nearly as complete.

Japanese	Kanji	Meaning
Some of the many words for tattooing		
Irezumi	入墨	blackening
Bunmi	文身	writing on the body
Shisei/ Tosei	刺青, 剳青	stabbing with blue
Kei/Gei	黥	facial tattooing
Keibatsu	黥罰	facial tattoo punishment
Keikei	黥刑	sentenced to facial tattooing
Bokukei	墨刑	ink punishment
Tensei	點青	spotted blue
Fusei	膚青	skin bluing
Horimono	彫物	engraving (tattoo)
Irebokuro	入贅	fake mole (tattoo)
Hori-ire	堀入	dig in (a tattoo)
Kisho-hori	起請彫	vow of love tattoo (both lovers have it)
Mon-mon	紋紋	design
Kurikara Mon-mon	倶利迦羅紋々	A tattoo of Lord Fudo taking the form of a dragon eating a sword.

Chapter	Page

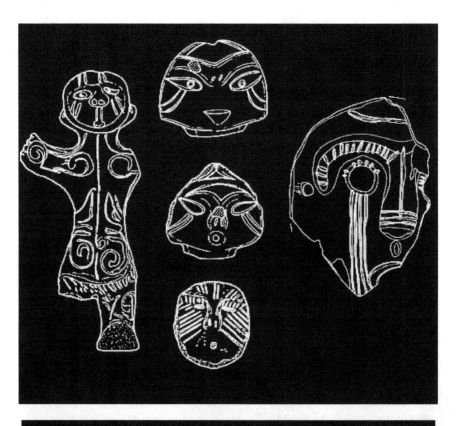

Jomon Era Tattooing

As Japan does not have a tradition of mummification it is nearly impossible to prove tattooing was done. However pottery depicting human figures unearthed from the Jomon Era, Japan's stone age 14,000 – 300 BCE, we can find some suggestions it was practiced. As the illustration below shows, early Jomon Era Japan was still connected by land bridges to what is modern day Russia and China. Eventually the oceans rose enough to cause Japan to become a series of four large and numerous smaller islands.

The pottery figures that archeologists uncovered all over Japan are called Dogu meaning "clay figure." Due to the markings on the faces of these Dogu, researchers theorized they may represent a culture of tattooing. This theory was first postulated by Hirai Seigoro but published by his student Yagi Sotaro in his 1902 book *Japanese Archeology*. Hirai/ Yagi initially concluded the figurines show two types of tattooing,

- covering the cheeks (right)
- connecting the eyebrows and around the mouth (left)

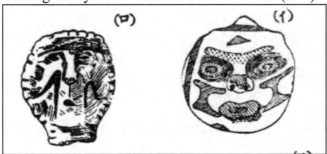

Later, Ono Nobutaro (1863-1938,) divided the markings into three categories and called them Geimen Dogu 黥面土偶, or clay figurines with facial tattoos. He divided the markings on the faces of the clay figurines into three categories,

● Cheek Tattooing
● Tattooing Around the Mouth
● Tattooing both on the Cheeks and Around the Mouth

Illustrations of various facial markings on clay figurines. *Culture in the Ground* 土中の文化:考古学研究資料 Ono Nobutaro, 1931.

He also brought up the issue that though the majority of the clay figurines appeared to be female, some had markings that could be interpreted either as beards or tattooing. The 15 illustrations above details some of these cases.

Several scholars at this time also noted that there could be other explanations for the markings from mundane make-up to ritual scarification. However, there seemed to be reluctant agreement that tattooing may well have been a major feature in Jomon Era Japanese culture. Mimori Sadao wrote in *Primitive Cultures of Japan* in 1931 that,

> *Since the clay figurines we find seem to have tattooing on them and this is in line with the descriptions in ancient sources. It is hard to dispute the fact that this tradition was carried out in some parts of the country. Modern Japan's stone age ancestors did all manner of teeth pulling, head shaping and every sort of body modification. It is hard to argue that there was no tattooing.*

Kono Isamu (1901 – 1967) expanded the categories of tattooing from 3 to 5. The illustrations are from his 1932 *A Critique of Facial Tattooing on Clay Figurines*.

1. Circles emanating from the mouth

2. Lines moving diagonally away from below the eyes

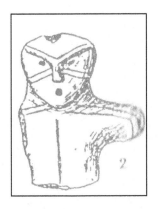

3. Tattooing around the mouth

4. Triangle at the left and right corner of the mouth pointing inward

5. Triangle at the left and right corner of the mouth pointing outward

Japanese Archeology contained the following illustrations divided by region. Some regional differences in facial tattooing/ scarification/ decoration can be seen.

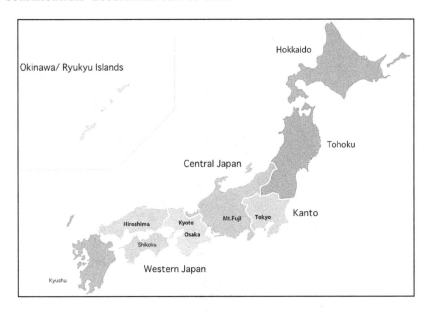

Western Japan

Central Japan

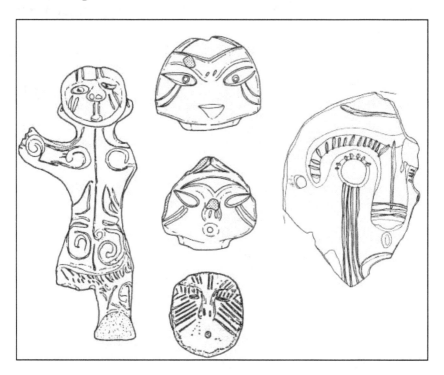

North Eastern Japan

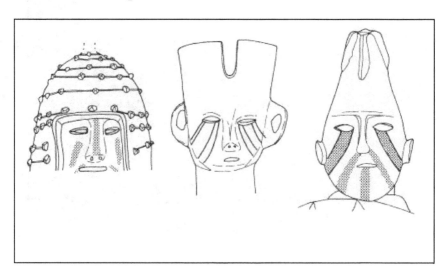

男子無大小皆黥其使詣中國、皆之子封於會稽、害。今倭水人好以厭大魚水禽、身各異、或左或有差。計其道里

Yayoi Era Tattooing
300 BCE – 300 CE

。自古以來、夫。夏后少康身以避蛟龍之魚蛤、文身亦爲飾。諸國文大或小、尊卑會稽、東冶之

Yayoi Era 300 BCE-300CE

The first recorded references to Japan and Japanese tattooing are in Chinese historical records starting in 57 CE when envoys were sent from the Later Han Dynasty. This section will introduce the ones that discuss tattooing, in chronological order. The first name given to Japan was "Wa," represented by the Kanji 倭, is the oldest recorded name for Japan. It was replaced by the Kanji 和 in the 8th century, which can also be read "Wa."

70 – 80 CE

The earliest mentions of Japan, referred to as Wa, are from Wang Chong's 1st century CE *Presentation of Philosophies of Religion and the Natural Sciences* 論衡.

The below passage describes, albeit vaguely, the Japanese people, called Woren 倭人. In this situation, envoys from Japan are in China presenting tribute. A discussion emerges of whether ancient bronze tripods had magic powers or not.

During the Chou time there was universal peace. An offering of white pheasants and Japanese odoriferous plants was made to the court. Someone commented that, "Since by eating a meal of these white pheasants and odoriferous plants will not keep one safe from evil spirits, why should vessels like bronze tripods have such a power?

-Adapted from Alfred Forke's 1907 translation *Philosophical Essays of Wang Ch'ung.*

82 CE

The Book of Han 漢書, primarily composed by Ban Gu 班固 covers the period 206 BCE-24 CE. It also briefly describes Japan.
Chinese text: 樂浪海中有倭人分爲百餘國
English translation:
Beyond the sea by Lo-lang, there are the people of Japan. They comprise more than one hundred communities.

22-220 CE

The Book of The Later Han 後漢書 edited by Fan Ye (398-445) 范曄, discusses the period from 25-220 CE. This book seems to be the first source that mentions tattooing among the Japanese people.

Chinese Text:

土宜禾稻、麻紵、蠶
桑，知織績為縑布。出
白珠、青玉。其山有丹
土。氣溫煖，冬夏生菜
茹。無牛馬虎豹羊鵲。
〔一〕其兵有矛、楯、木
弓，竹矢或以骨為鏃。
男子皆黥面文身，以其
文左右大小別尊卑之
差。其男衣皆橫幅結束
相連。女人被髮屈紒，
衣如單被，貫頭而著之
並以丹朱坋身，〔二〕如
中國之用粉也。有城柵
屋室。

English Translation:

The local soil was suitable for growing rice, linen, and mulberry. The Wa people knew the skill of weaving. The place also produced white pearls and green jade. There was red soil on the local mountains. The local climate was mild and warm. Vegetables grew in both summer and winter. There were no cattle, tigers, leopards, sheep, or magpies. The local people used spears, shields and wooden bows as weapons. They may also use bones as arrow heads. All men wore tattoos over the face and the body. They distinguished ranks through the size and the locations of the tattoos they wore. The garment for local men was a piece of cloth wrapped around the body and tied. The women wore long shaggy hair. Their clothes resemble a thin quilt, with a hole through which the head penetrated to put on the piece of cloth. The women also applied red powder onto the body, a way similar with the practice by the people in the Central Plain. There were also city walls and residential houses.

280 CE

The next mention of tattooing in Japan occurs in the *Records of Wei* 魏志 which is part of a larger historical work called *The Records of the Three Kingdoms* 三国志. The work, written by Chen Shou 陳壽 covers from 184- 280 CE and overlaps *The Book of The Later Han.* The specific section is called *Barbarians of the East: Wajin* 東夷傳倭人. This is typically referred to as *The Story of the Wajin in Records of Wei* 魏志倭人伝 in Japan, probably because the former title is fairly derogatory.

A country called Nu 奴國 is described. Tsunoda Ryusaku suggests in *Japan in Chinese Dynastic Histories*, 1951, this country is the southern part of Kyushu island. The Kanji for this area 奴國 translates to "slave country." It is also later referred to as Dog Slave Country 狗奴國 and is located 12,000 Chinese leagues south of Wa. This seems to indicate the area is where the ancient Kumaso people of Kyushu lived.

Chinese text:

> 男子無大小皆自
> 黥面文身。
> 古以來、其使自
> 詣中國、皆自
> 稱大夫。夏后
> 少康之子封於
> 會稽、斷髮文
> 身以避蛟龍之
> 害。今倭人
> 好沈沒捕魚
> 蛤、文身亦以
> 厭大魚水禽、
> 後稍以爲飾。
> 諸國文身各
> 異、或左或右、
> 或大或小、尊
> 卑有差。計其
> 道里、當在會
> 稽、東冶之東。

English translation:

Men of all social rank tattoo their faces and bodies with designs. Even in days long past, envoys from Japan who visited the Chinese Court referred to themselves as "men of high standing." The son of Shao Kang, the sixth king of the Xia Dynasty, cut his hair and decorated his body with designs in order to protect himself from attacks by serpents and dragons when he was crowned lord of Kuaiji.

The Japanese, who are known to dive into the ocean to harvest various kinds of fish and shellfish, also tattoo their bodies. Originally this was done in order to protect against sharks and predatory water fowl, however this tradition has evolved into tattooing as body decoration. Depending on the region the tattooing can be on the left side or right, be very large or be small. Japan is many leagues to the east of Kuaiji.

– Records of Wei 297 CE

The above passage notes both the origins and current state of tattooing in the Japanese islands. It also notes a correlation with the Chinese culture of kings tattooing themselves when they ascended to the throne. The Xia dynasty is a legendary dynasty that existed around 2070 BCE–1600 BCE.

239-265 CE

In the same Era *An Abbreviated History of Wei* 魏略 by Yu Huan (220–265) states that,

Chinese text:

```
女王之南、又有狗奴國、
女（以）男子爲王、其官曰
拘右（古）智卑狗、不屬女
王也。自帯方至女（一闕
「王」）國萬二千餘里。其
俗男子皆點（黥面）而文
〔闕「身」）、聞其舊語、自
謂太伯之後、昔夏后少康
之子、封於會稽、斷髮文
身以避蛟龍之吾（害）。今
〔亻妾〕倭）人亦文身、以厭
水害也。自帯方至女国萬
二千余里其俗男子皆点
而文聞其旧語自謂太伯
之後昔夏后少康之子封
於会稽断髮文身以避蛟
龍之害今倭人又文身以
厭水害也
```

English translation:

To the south of the area ruled by the queen (probably referring to Himiko 卑弥呼 170-248 CE,) *there is the Slave Dog Country. They are ruled by a king. He is known as Kouchi Hiko* 狗古智卑狗. *That country has no association with the queen.*

The distance from the main cities in China to the area ruled by the queen is some twenty thousand leagues. All men in this area have tattoos in various places on their bodies. If you ask them the

origin of the markings they invariably reply that they are meant to show deference to Taihaku.(The legendary 12th Century BCE founder of the Kingdom of Wu).

Long ago in the kingdom Xia, when the son of Shao Kang, the sixth king of the Xia dynasty 2070 – 1600 BCE, was crowed as lord of Kuaiji, cut his hair and decorated his body with designs in order to avoid the attack of serpents and dragons. These days Japanese tattoo themselves to stay safe in the water.

Several Japanese scholars interpreted the tattooing done by these early Japanese as primarily a protective measure. The aquatic lifestyle they lead required them to repeatedly dive to great depths to catch fish and harvest abalone. Entering those deep, dark depths could be a frightening, dangerous business as demons dwelled in the deep, therefore the tattoos were done in order to defend the Japanese of this era as they worked. In other words, the tattooing was done as part of a religious ceremony in order to obtain supernatural protection. This was the main goal of the tattooing done by the Japanese at that time.

The anthropologist Torii Ryuzo 鳥居龍蔵 (1870-1953) emphasized in his *Tattooing Amongst the Early Japanese*:

Though originally it was done as part of their religious practice and conferred spiritual power it later evolved into body decoration. I believe researchers of the Wajin (Japanese) tattooing done at this time must focus their research on this transition.

He continues,

The designs that they engrave into their flesh serve as charms or talismans against evil spirits....and this brings up an interesting point. If the Japanese at this time used tattooing talismans to ward of demons from the deep sea, what form did they take?

Since there is no tradition of mummification in Japan, it is difficult to determine how the tattooing looked. Neither the *Records of Wei* nor *An Abbreviated History of Wei* describe the tattooing with any detail.

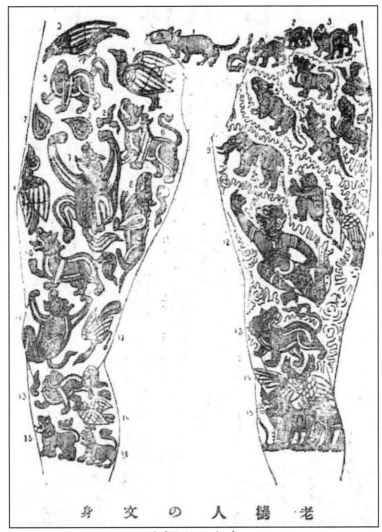

老樅人の文身

The anthropologist Torii Ryuzo 鳥居龍蔵 （1870-1953）included this illustration of the tattooed legs of a person from Laos in *Tattooing Amongst the Early Japanese*. The tattoos are all numbered however Ryuzo did not include a corresponding description. The sheer number and variety of tattoos in this illustration is impressive. The wavy "power waves" emanating off the creatures on the right hand side seem to generally be driving away the creatures on the left.

Torii seems to be saying this could be the style of tattooing done by the early Japanese. He notes that while the *Records of Wei* states:

When the son of King Shao Kang was crowed as lord of Kuaiji, he cut his hair and decorated his body with designs in order to avoid the attack of serpents and dragons.

That passage is then followed by a brief introduction to the tattooing done by the Japanese:

The Japanese, who are known to dive into the ocean to harvest various kinds of fish and shellfish, also tattoo their bodies.

However, in *The Records of the Grand Historian Book* 太史公書史記 by Sima Qian in 94 BCE, one passage describes the tradition of shaving the head and tattooing the body by people living in the coastal regions of China. A footnote to that section by Ying Shao 應劭 (140 – 206 CE) makes the observation that,

They spend a great deal of time in the water. They shave their heads and tattoo the bodies with dragons and in this way protect themselves from danger.

While there is not a great deal to be found in the pages of *The Records of the Grand Historian,* only the passage...*tattoo the bodies with dragons and in this way protect themselves from danger*... is significant. Here we can determine that the tattooing is of dragons. On the other hand, the description in the *Records of Wei* unfortunately makes no mention of tattooing.

The Japanese, who are known to dive into the ocean to harvest various kinds of fish and shellfish, also tattoo their bodies. Originally this was done in order to protect against sharks and predatory water fowl, however this tradition has evolved into tattooing as body decoration.

Torii Ryuzo evaluates this as follows,

However, <u>The Records of the Grand Historian</u> mentions the people in the coastal areas tattoo themselves with dragons. Therefore it is entirely possible the early Japanese also tattooed themselves with dragons. As to why they chose dragons the answer is that the dragon is thought of as the king of the underwater realm. It is interesting to speculate on the implications of a common thread of dragon tattooing amongst costal Chinese, southeast Asians and the early Japanese.

635 CE

The Book of Liang 梁書 covers the history of the Liang Dynasty 502-557. There are two sections dealing with Japan, still referred to as Wa.

Chinese text:

倭者自云太伯之後俗皆文身去帶方萬二千餘里

English translation:

The Japanese consider themselves to be descendants of Taibo, the 12 C. BCE founder of the Kingdom of Wu. The people all tattoo themselves. Their territory is about 20,000 Chinese Leagues (1,500 kilometers) from our realm

Chinese text:

文身國在倭國東北
七千餘里人體有文
如獸其額上有三文
文直者貴文小者賤
土俗歡樂物豐而賤
行客不齎糧有屋宇
無城郭其王所居
飾以金銀珍麗繞屋
爲塹廣一丈實以水
銀雨則流于水銀之
上市用珍寶犯輕罪
者則鞭杖犯死罪則
置猛獸食之有枉則
猛獸避而不食經宿
則赦之

English translation:

The country of Wenshen is 7,000 Chinese Leagues north-east of the country of Wa. Over their body, they have tattoos depicting wild beasts. They have three tattooed marks on their foreheads. The marks are straight for noble people and are small for lowly people. The people like music, but are not very generous in spite of their affluence, and do not give anything to strangers.

They have houses, but no castles. The place in which their king resides is decorated with gold and silver in a manner of rare beauty. The buildings are surrounded by a ditch, about one cho in width, which they fill with quicksilver (mercury.) When there is rain, it flows on top of the quicksilver.

They have many rare things in their markets.

Those who are guilty of a light offences are immediately punished with leather whips. Normally, the historian relates, to punish crimes they use whipping, but for crimes deserving of capital punishment, they throw the offender to fierce wild animals to be eaten alive. If the person is innocent the beasts will avoid him, and if he remains unharmed overnight he will be pardoned. Crimes can also be redeemed through imprisonment without food.

- Translation from *Early Chinese Tattoo* by Carrie E. Reed 2000. Sino-Platonic Papers

636 CE

Finally, *The Book of Sui* 隋書, a Chinese history book completed in 636 CE, states the following about the early Japanese,

Chinese text:

男女多黥臂點面文身没水捕魚

English translation:

Both men and women have numerous tattoos from the elbow to the upper arm and tattooed markings on their faces.

Dragons

Dragons are mentioned frequently in the previous passages and below are two early examples of dragon illustrations. The oldest illustration of a dragon appears to be *Silk Painting Depicting a Man Riding a Dragon* 人物御龍帛畫.

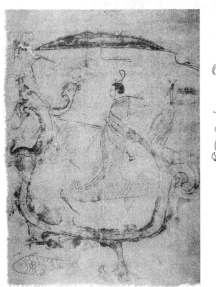 

The artist and exact date are unclear but it was found in a tomb in the 1970's and dated to the Warring States Period (475-221 BCE). The drawing shows a regal figure controlling a dragon. Since a fish is drawn below, this seems to imply the man is going through or under the sea, rather than through the air. In addition the bird perched on the back of the dragon recalls the various passages from the *Book of Wei*. Though the dragon is almost completely encircling the figure, he remains in a position of control.

A later illustration also features numerous figures controlling dragons. The illustration is titled *Aerial Contest of Dragon-Chariot and Dragon-Riders* and dates from the Han Era 147 CE. It is a line drawing of a stone bas-relief from the Field Museum of Natural History. One figure rides in a chariot pulled by a set of four dragons. One driver has the reins and two attendants follow mounted on their own dragons. Several bird-like figures appear as well.

Aerial Contest of Dragon-Chariot and Dragon-Riders 147 CE

Early Japanese Texts

660 BCE

Kojiki 古事記 The Record of Ancient Matters 1

Kojiki 古事記, or *Record of Ancient Matters* is the first history of Japan, completed in 713. One episode that involves tattoos occurred around 660 BCE. It features a character named 大久米命 Okume no Mikoto. Okume served as a kind of bodyguard to the Emperor Jinmu 711-585 BCE. It was Emperor Jinmu who brought the Japanese people to Nara and established the Yamato kingdom, defeating the local tribes in the process. In this passage Okume no Mikoto introduces a girl to the emperor:

"One day seven girls came to play in the fields around Takasajino, amongst them was a girl named Isuke Yori Hime. Okume saw her and asked the emperor in song:

Lord of Yamato born in Takasajino, seven girls have appeared before you, which of them does my lord choose?

A girl by the name of Isuke Yori Hime was standing nearest of the group. The emperor saw the girl because she was standing closest and answered Okume in song:

The one standing closest to me has already captured my heart. They all of course are very beautiful.

Hearing his lord's response Okume went over to the girl and extended an invitation from the emperor. Isuke Yori Hime looked at Okume and was startled by his unusual appearance. He had tattoos around his eyes that made them look sharp and quite avian in appearance. She sang:

May I ask why you have sharply defined eyes like those of the fork tailed swift, oriental cuckoo, plover and quail?

Okume answered her in song:

I thought I might be better able to find you and meet you if I had large sharp eyes."

-Translated from *The Kojiki in Modern Japanese* 現代語訳古事記 1943 by Ueki Naoichiro 植木直一郎 1878-1959.

This is the first mention of tattooing in Japanese literature. The tattooing is called Sakerutome 黥利目 or "tattooing to sharpen the eyes." Ueki Naoichrio writes the Kanji as 裂ける鋭眼 or "sharp split at the eyes." Another rendering of the Kanji replaces the first character with "tattooing" 黥 with similar looking "whale"鯨. This could be a transcription error, however the word *sakeru* means to avoid and the word *tome* means to stop. Assembling the meaning of the Kanji together could leave us with "eyes that stop the whales."

Artist's rendering of Sakerutome tattooing around the eyes.

Yasuda Tokutaro 安田徳太郎 is more straightforward with his analysis of the tattooing described in the Kojiki in his *Japanese Tattooing Customs* 1952.

Tattooing in Japan is a holdover from traditions brought north by people living in the southern pacific. Many of these countries tattoo the whole body. When they travelled north long ago, they found the uninhabited Japanese islands and made their home. These are the people first encountered by the Chinese. The tradition of tattooing continued as these people from the south pacific gradually became what we know as the Hayato of southern Kyushu. Even today we can see the peoples of the south pacific tattoo themselves extensively.
Because Okume was Hayato, he had extensive tattooing.

97 CE

Nihon Shoki 日本書紀 *The Chronicles of Japan* 1

The *Nihon Shoki* or *The Chronicles of Japan*, is the second earliest book on Japanese history. It covers the creation of the islands of Japan as the Kojiki does, but with more detail and continues its account up until the 8th century. The following sections discuss tattooing in early Japan. This first passage discusses an envoy's encounter with tribes in the eastern area of Japan.

Japanese Text:

二十七年春二月辛丑朔壬子。武内宿禰自東國還之奏言。東夷之中。有日高見國。其國人。男女並椎結文身。為人勇悍。是総曰蝦夷。亦土地沃壤而曠之。可取也。撃

English Translation:

27th year, Spring, 2nd month, 12th day (97 CE.)
Takechi no Sukune returned from the East Country and informed the Emperor saying,

In the Eastern wilds there is a country called Hitakami. The people of this country, both men and women, tie up their hair in the form of a mallet, and tattoo their bodies. They are of a fierce temper, and their general name is Yemishi. Moreover, their land is wide and fertile. We should attack them and take it.

-Translation by W. G. Aston

Tanaka Kogai discusses this in *History of Tattooing*. He feels this is evidence that other than the tribes in the northeast and in the southern Kyushu and Ryukyu islands, tattooing was not widely practiced in Japan.

Thus it can be seen that the true Japanese people, the descendants of the gods, those that immigrated from the Chinese and Mongolian lands did not engage in tattooing. In fact tattooing the face 黥 and tattooing lettering on the body 文身 was anathema to them.

399 CE

Nihonshoki 日本書紀 *The Chronicles of Japan* 2

There is a reference to tattooing as punishment in the chapter for Emperor Nintoku 仁徳天皇(313–399.) In the year 399, a man named Azumi no Hamako 阿曇浜子 who supported an insurrection led by Prince Suminoe no Nakatsu 住吉仲 was sentenced to tattooing. Below is the section that talks about Azumi no Hamako being given a death sentence but having it commuted to facial tattooing.

Passage from Nihonshoki	Transcription of the passage
	元年春二月壬午朔、皇太子即位於磐余稚櫻宮。 夏四月辛巳朔丁酉、召阿雲連濱子、詔之曰「汝、與仲皇子共謀逆、將傾国家、罪當于死。然、垂大恩而兔死科墨。」 卽日黥之、因此、時人曰阿雲目。

Page from *Chronicles of Japan* discussing tattooing.

English Translation:

"On April 17th in the first year of his reign, the emperor summoned Azumi no Muraji Hamako into his presence. It was summer by the old calendar. He said,

You met with Nakatsu and plotted a rebellion against the nation. For this crime you are sentenced to death! However, since I owe you a debt I will pardon you and only demand that your face be tattooed.

And thus on that day the punishment of *Hitahi Kizamu Tsumi* 墨 or a "Crime to be Punished" by Engraving the Forehead, was carried out." From that time on *Mesaki-kiza* 黥, or tattooing around the eyes became known as *Azumi-me* 阿曇目, or Like the Eyes of Azumi." Somewhat confusingly the tattooing is called "Engraving the Forehead" but most interpret this as "Tattooing the edges of the eyes." 目の縁に入れ墨をした.

Interestingly the blog, *Japanese Age of Legends*, has the following interpretation of this section:

These seafaring people already had facial tattooing. The tattooing was not due to an order given by the Emperor, rather it was a tradition practiced by these seafaring people. Reference to this can be found in 魏志倭人伝. The Yamato region of central Japan cultivated rice as the basis of their civilization. The seafaring people who lived in the south west as well as the hunter tribes of the north (the Ainu as well as on the Korean peninsula) also had a different focus to their culture.

These different tribes, mixed and fought and made peace over and over again, eventually forming the Japanese culture. How then did the Japanese deal with the rather unusual culture of the seafaring people? The answer could be that the "Azumi-me punishment" was no more than a rumor to cover the cultural difference. During this period, Azumi served as a representative of one area of the domain. In other words a supporter of the Imperial Throne. Despite being involved in the machinations just before the succession to the throne the Emperor could not punish him, despite the fact that he supported the other side. This is because he was the representative for an entire region. In the end he probably was not punished at all.

-Translation of nihonshinwa.com

404 CE

Nihonshoki 日本書紀 *The Chronicles of Japan* 3

Dr. Tanaka sites as further evidence of this distain for tattooing by the Japanese also in *The Chronicles of Japan.* The section detailing Emperor Richu's (336 - 405 CE) hunting trip to Awaji.

秋九月(ながづき)乙酉(きのととのとり)朔壬寅(みづのえとらのひ)天皇(すめらみこと)狩于淡路嶋(あはじのしま)是日 河内飼部(かふちのうまかひべ)等 從駕(おほみともに)つかへる)執轡(おほみまのくちにつける) 先是 飼部(うまかひべ)之黥(めさきのきず)皆未差(いえる) 時居嶋伊奘諾神(いざなきのかみ) 託(かかる)祝(はふり)曰(のたまふ)不堪血臭矣 因以 卜(うらなふ)之 兆(うらはひ)云 惡(にくむ)飼部等黥之氣(か)故自是以後 頓(ひたぶる)絶以不黥(めさきす)飼部而止之癸卯(みづのとのうのひ)

Map showing the location of Awaji Island.

The horse handlers 馬飼部 ウマカイベ *from the Kawauchi Region, who were in charge of the animals that pulled the Emperor's caravan had tattoos that were not yet healed. Finding himself unable to bear the stench of blood the Emperor concluded that the reason the cuts did not heal was that it was an oracle from the Shinto deity Izanagi 伊弉諾 or "He-Who-Invites" who resides in Awaji. He decreed that henceforth handlers of beasts should be forbidden from tattooing themselves.*

Dr. Tanaka's interpretation of this passage is as follows:

Considering the fact that the smell of blood was anathema to the people descended from the goddess Ama Terasu Oomi Kami it goes without saying that they did not do any tattooing of their own. The animal handlers who were tattooed were part of a completely separate people, of Wajin decent, and not associated with the divine people.

The last line of his statement indicates that he does not consider the Wajin first encountered by the Chinese envoys to be Japanese.

450 CE

Kojiki 古事記 The Record of Ancient Matters 2

The second passage from Kojiki that mentions tattoos takes place during the reign of Emperor Ankou (453-456 C.E.) describing the flight of two members of the royal family, princes Ohoke and Woke:

Japanese Text:

於是、市邊王之
王子等、意祁王・
袁祁王二柱聞此
亂而逃去。
故到山代苅羽
井、食御粮之時、
面黥老人來、奪
其粮。爾其二王
言「不惜粮。」
然汝者誰人。」答
曰「我者山代之猪
甘也。」故逃渡玖
須婆之河、至針
間國、入其國人
名志自牟之家、
隱身、役於馬甘
牛甘也

English Translation:

Hereupon King Ichi-no-be's children King Ohoke and King Woke (two Deities), having heard of this affray, fled away. So when they reached Karibawi in Yamashiro and were eating their august provisions, an old man with a tattooed face came and seized the provisions. Then the two Kings said:
"We do not grudge the provisions. But who art thou? "
He replied, saying: "I am a boar-herd in Yamashiro."

-From *The Kojiki*, translated by Basil Hall Chamberlain, 1919, at sacred-texts.com

Again we have a person involved with raising animals having a facial tattoo, here written with two Kanji 面黥 the first meaning "face" and the second "facial tattooing."

467 CE

Nihonshoki 日本書紀 *The Chronicles of Japan* 4

Another early example of tattoos as punishment can be found under the entry for Emperor Yuryaku 雄略天皇 (418 - 479.) The story is about the emperor's response to a hunting bird being killed by a dog.

Japanese Text:

冬十月、鳥官之
禽、爲菟田人狗所
嚙死。天皇瞋、黥面
而爲鳥養部。於是、
信濃国直丁與武藏
国直丁、侍宿、相謂
曰「嗟乎、我国積鳥
之高、同於小墓。旦
暮而食、尚有其餘。
今天皇、由一鳥之
故而黥人面、太無
道理、惡行之主
也。」天皇聞而使聚
積之、直丁等不能
忽備、仍詔爲鳥養
部。

English Translation:

"Events during a wintery October in the 11th year of Emperor Yuryaku's rule, 467 CE.

A hunting bird under the care of the falconer was mauled to death by one of the dogs of a man from Uda (modern Nara). The Emperor was furious this would be allowed to happen and sentenced him to Keimen, a facial tattoo, and thereby demoting him to the rank/social status of Torikaibe, a person who raises birds for food.

That evening the squires from Shinano (today's Nagano Prefecture) and Musashi (today's Tokyo) happened to be taking lodging in the same inn and they talked of these events that evening.

Birds in my country are so numerous that if you were to catch them all and stack them, the mound would be as big as a Kofun tomb mound.

Ha-ha! If you ate them every morning and every night you would still have some left over. And today the Emperor lost one bird

so he decided to tattoo a man on his face! This is appalling and unconscionable. What a terrible ruler!
The Emperor overhearing this said,
Is that true about the number of birds? You squires, immediately gather them all!

The squires were unable to gather every bird in the land and were demoted to Torikaibe.

Emperor Yuryaku died at the age of 124. This episode indicates that people working with animals were either tattooed to indicate that status or tattooing was done amongst themselves. This tradition seems to have continued despite the fact that Emperor Richu's (336 - 405 CE)

Divisions of Society System

The early histories of Japan frequently mention people involved with the care of animals as being tattooed. Further, the tattooing seems to have been on the face.

What all these groups have in common is they were part of what was called the Beminsei 部民制, or Divisions of Society System. The system, which was used in the Yamato Period from around 250-670 CE, divided the populous into groups responsible for different work.

The groups that dealt with raising animals had names that reflected the animals they were in charge of. This was then followed by the word Kaibe (pronounced Kai-Beh) using the Kanji 飼部, meaning "raising (animal husbandry) group." In this case it seems to be closer in meaning to caste.

It seems likely that those born into such a group stayed within that group. In addition, people that displeased their lords could be relegated to this caste, as a form of punishment. This was done in conjunction with facial tattooing. The early Chinese sources indicate the Japanese they encountered living near the water, tattooed themselves with water creatures, both real and imagined. It is interesting to consider whether this applied to the other animal castes and whether these casts were all considered to be the same or if there were ranks, according to the type of animal.

Below is a list of the different jobs that dealt with animals and therefore possibly also meant that the members were tattooed to a degree.

Kanji	Reading	Job
鶏飼部	*Torikaibeh*	Raising birds for food. However, the person in charge of the care of Taka, or hawks, for hunting seems to have been a higher ranked position called Torikan 鳥官, or bird official.
馬飼部	*Umakaibeh*	Raising horses Also written simply as 飼部
牛飼部	*Ushikaibeh*	Raising cattle
水飼部	*Mizukaibeh*	Brings water to horses or livestock
犬養部	*Inukaibeh*	Breeding and training dogs for guarding or hunting
猪飼部	*Ikaibeh*	Raising wild boar
海部	*Kaibeh*	Also read as Ama, people that spearfish and collect shellfish
The words can also be written with 甘 or 養 instead of 飼		

The Beminsei lasted until 670, after which people were grouped by family register. The Beminsei names became the family name of the associated people. Even today Japanese people with the above listed names can be found. There are no specifics regarding the tattooing done by these groups, however some information regarding protective symbols of the Ama remain.

Ama : Male and Female Divers

The early Chinese books that discuss the Japanese archipelago and Japanese tattooing all mention how Japanese spent a great deal of time in the water collecting fish and shellfish. While there is no tradition of mummification, this arduous physical activity does leave evidence. This is because people that spend a great deal of time in the water develop a condition known as exostosis of the external auditory canal 外耳道外骨腫 or more known as "surfer's ear." It affects people spending time in cold water and wind.

According to the Palo Alto Medical Foundation website,

Cooling of the ear canal stimulates bone growth that narrows the canal and blocks the eardrum. This narrowing traps water and earwax in the canal, often resulting in painful ear infections and hearing loss.

Yoshioka Ikuo writes in his *Anthropology of Tattooing* that this condition has been found in Jomon and Yayoi era skeletons. Therefore, one aspect of what was written in the Chinese texts can be corroborated.

The tradition of open ocean diving to gathering seafood and pearls never ended in Japan. Particularly in the Izu peninsula, but active all over Japan are the Ama, divers. The word Ama, written as 海女 Sea Girl, if they are women or, 海士 Sea Knight, if they are men, refers to people that dove for seafood. While the name "Ama" dates from the Heian Era 794-1185, clearly this tradition also existed from the days of the Divisions of Society System.

Even today there are some 2000 female Ama continuing to harvest abalone (according to a 2010 survey by the Japan Ocean Museum.) While modern Ama wear wetsuits, up through the 1930s the women wore only a loin-cloth with a headscarf when diving. Since they dive repeatedly into the ocean, descending into deeper colder water and spend time underwater prying creatures off rocks and teasing them out of crevices, Ama are known to suffer from surfer's ear. Though the tradition of tattooing does not remain their headscarves are embroidered with lucky and protective symbols, which certainly recall the much earlier tradition. The following symbols are used by the Ama.

Protective Symbols Used by the Ama

Seimei 清明
The Seimei was introduced in the Heian Era by the Abe no Seimei 安倍晴明 921-1005. He was an Onmyoji 陰陽師, a kind of astrologer/ sorcerer. Onmyoji held official positions in the emperor's cabinet as civil servants. They devised calendars and advised on the spiritually correct way to handle matters of state. Abe no Seimei enjoyed an extremely long life, free from any major illness, which contributed to the popular belief that he had mystical powers.

    [The duties of Onmyoji] *included analyzing strange events, conducting exorcisms, warding against evil spirits, and performing various rites of geomancy. He was said to be especially skilled in divining the sex of fetuses and finding lost objects.* Miller, Laura. *Extreme Makeover for a Heian-era Wizard. Mechademia 3: Limits of the Human.* U. of Minnesota Press, 2008.

Kagome 籠目
The Kagome or basket weave is a symbol of protection since it forms a hexagram 六芒星 called *Rokubohsei* in Japanese.

Manji 卍
The Manji was first used in India in the Neolithic Era 12,000 years ago. The Hindu religion sees it as the swirl in the center of the God Vishnu's chest. Buddhism interprets the Manji as signifying the approach of a blessing or good fortune.

Doman 道満

This symbol is known as Doman. It was also said to have been developed by an Onmyoji named Ashiya Doman 蘆屋道満 who lived at the same time as (and was possibly a rival to) Abe no Seimei. This symbol is also used in **Kuji-kiri 九字切り** or nine symbolic cuts in Esoteric Buddhism. The below 19th century illustration describes this spiritual ritual. The fingers represent a cutting sword with each line cutting the air in a specific order, representing a certain symbol and deity.

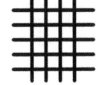

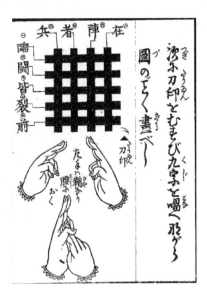

鱗 Uroko

This simple triangle represents Uroko or fish scales. In Japanese textiles it is often compounded into patterns.

592-1603 CE Abandonment of Tattooing?

Many Japanese scholars point out that in the 1000 year period 592-1603, starting in the reign Empress Suiko all the way through the Momoyama Era, there are virtually no documents that mention tattooing. Therefore they conclude that in this period tattooing was not done. Indeed Tanaka states that,

If you consider these early Japanese texts as a whole, it is clear that Japan had already done away with tattooing by the time our nation began negotiating treaties with other nations. Thus by the time of the reign of Empress Suiko (592-628CE) it had been eliminated from our culture. Further, beginning in the following Asuka Fujiwara Era (694-710) and extending through the Nara (710-794) and Heian Eras (794-1185) there are almost no historical documents or references to tattooing.

There are some notable exceptions, the first being the tradition of tattooing in northeastern Japan by the Ainu and second by the peoples of the Ryukyu islands, now called the Okinawan Islands. In addition in the 30 volume book *Buddhism in the Genko Era* published in 1322, there is a chapter called Ninko 忍行 or *Path of Endurance*. The entries in this book describe monks that have tattooed their bodies with religious themed symbols and text.

A simple line drawing of the Amitabh Celestial Buddha from *Illustrations of All Sects of Buddhism. Edo Era.*

For example, there is a passage that mentions Sha Sen Mei, a monk who was born in the Domain of Awa. Sha Sen Mei was devoted to travelling around Japan doing intensive spiritual training. He had tattooed the Amitabh Celestial Buddha across his back. Another monk, by the name of Sha Shin Kei had tattooed the back of his hands and tops of his feet with images of Kannon and the Celestial Buddha. Writers like Tanaka Kogai tend to dismiss the notion that this was evidence of a "tattooing culture" and instead characterize it as limited to certain religious sects. He states,

Though there are examples of monks tattooing themselves dating from the time of the Heian Court through the beginning of the Kamakura Era (794-1333), for the most part this tattooing was done by themselves or at their bequest as part of their Kugyo, ritual mortification of the flesh.

So, despite a tattooing tradition among Buddhist adherents extending for 500 years, Tanaka dismisses it as an aberration.

The next written record of tattooing does not occur until 1587. The book *Intoku Taiheiki* 陰徳太平記 is a record of events from the 16th century that was published in 1717. On February 7th of 1587 there is an entry regarding Kyushu. Toyotomi Hideyoshi dispatched General Yamato Hidenaga as part of his plan to subjugate the Kyushu island. The reason was the Shimazu family had been steadily advancing northward and were on the cusp of controlling the whole island of Kyushu.

Hidenaga arrived in Hyuga Domain with over 90,000 soldiers and surrounded Takajo Castle. The Satsuma forces were significantly outnumbered, but Shimazu Toshihisa lead a group of 20,000 soldiers in an attack. Though they fought with vigor the Shimazu forces were eventually forced to withdraw. Before beginning their retreat they left a unit of 500 men behind to delay pursuit. This famous tactic, known as the Shimazu Escape, involved leaving Samurai that were expected to fight to the death in order to buy time for the main force to gain distance.

When the forces of Hidenaga were reviewing the bodies of the five hundred Satsuma Samurai that were killed, they were startled to find all 500 had tattoos on their arms. The writing clearly said,

"On February 7th [name] was cut down in battle."

Tanaka had the following to say about this,

This was a testament to the bravery of these soldiers. The Samurai of the Satsuma area are known as Satsuma-Hayato, meaning they are Wajin descended from Hayato tribe people. From times long past they have a tradition of tattooing that it seems to have extended almost to the Momoyama Era (which began in 1573.) Therefore, other than the abovementioned Samurai of the Satsuma Domain, it seems we can find no real sign or mention of tattooing up through the end of the Momoyama Era 1573-1600.

In fact, in the book titled <u>The Fun Happy Laughing Reader</u> by Kitamura Nobuyo it states, "Though there were many villains and rough looking men you never heard of anyone being covered in tattoos. Later all variety of customer came calling but none could be said to have any tattoos."

The Japanese researchers do seem to spend a lot of time discounting vast swaths of people with a tattooing culture. The Ainu in the north, the Ryukyu (now Okinawa) Islands in the south, the Hayato and religious practitioners. However, starting the early 17th century tattooing began to re-emerge.

The Re-emergence of Tattooing

Vows of Love

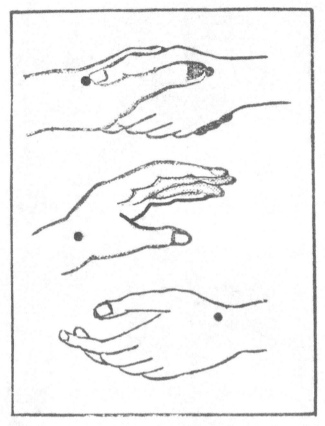

ろくぼ入の約誓女男

Illustration of the "promise mole" tattoo from *The Hundred Shapes of Tattoos* by Tamabayashi Haruo.

The earliest tattoos in the 1600s seem to have been Iribokuro, or engraved moles. These were simple tattoos that could be confused with a naturally occurring mole and were self-applied. They were done as a kind of a promise between lovers. A spot would be tattooed at the base of the thumb right at the spot the other lover's thumb naturally stopped. When the couple held hands the thumb would rest just on the Iribokuro. The early 20th century researcher, Tamabayashi Haruo, describes these as "vows of love."

In the Kanei Era 1624-1645, stories of tattooing suddenly begin to appear in literature. An early example of this can be found in the sixth volume of *Great Mirror of the Erotic Way* 1680. In a passage discussing prostitutes the following passage appears,

Around the time of Kanei, in a shop known as Nomaya in Osaka there was a prostitute of the second-highest class by the name of Sakuya Joro. She had two very good customers whose names began with the number seven, or Shichi. They were Mr. Shichi-ro Uemon and Mr. Shichi-be. On the front of her shoulder she had tattooed the phrase My Life for My Lord Seven *(which could refer to either man.) I can't imagine why she thought showing this tattoo to either man would bring them joy. It seems a strange way to serve indeed.*

Tattooing gradually began to be adopted by young "star crossed lovers." In Japan Shinchu 心中, or "to be madly in love," gave rise to all manner of demonstrations of love. Shaving your head, pulling out your own fingernails, cutting off the last joint of a finger and even double suicides were not unknown. Tattooing became part of this tradition.

Tanaka Kogai describes this in *History of Tattooing*:

At that time the practice of tattooing a name or carving a vow into the flesh was done by courtesans in order to encourage customers. The procedure was for the man to dip a brush in ink and write his name on the woman's skin. The woman would then use a razor to incise the flesh, thereby pushing the ink into the skin. Later needles were found to deliver a better result and they replaced razors.

The process was to abbreviate a name and then write it in the simpler Katakana alphabet. If the man's name was Kanbei then "Kan" followed by the honorific title "Sama" would be written. A sole Kanji "my life"命 would be placed at the end. The final tattoo would be etched in with a razor as *My Life for My Lord Kan* カンサマ命. The name Kurobei would be rendered as *My Life for My Lord Kuro* クロサマ命.

That Must Really Hurt: Irezumi. By 芳年 Yoshitoshi 1888.

Numbers were used frequently in Japanese names during this era and these were handle playfully. One example is the name Jubei, which has the Kanji for "ten 十" written first. This could be rendered cleverly as *My Life for Two Fives* 二五命. Similarly Kyubei, which starts with the Kanji for "nine 九" would be tattooed as *My Life for Three by Three* 三三命.

The placement of these tattoos could be on the right or left arm. In the novels *The Great Mirror of Male Love* and the later *Yamato*

Decorative Mirror have the tattoos predominately on the left arm, while the *Expansive Collection of Illustrated Examples* has it on the right arm. The positioning was typically on the middle of the upper part of the arm on the outside, however as *The Great Mirror of Male Love* indicates the area ranging from the outside the shoulder to as far as the elbow could be tattooed. There are also references to women tattooing the names of male lovers between their fingers.

Though this tradition was mostly practiced by the brothel workers in the Kyoto and Osaka areas, it clearly originated in an earlier era. The fact that this kind of tattooing was also being done by homosexual men in this period can be confirmed in the following passage from the book *Violent Dog Collection* written in the tenth year of Kanei 1634.

Amongst the younger crowd there is an unnecessary tattooing of the flesh.

Another entry in the pages of the *Great Mirror of the Erotic Way* talks of how a courtesan in the Shimahara section of Kyoto had the names of male customers tattooed onto her arms. She even tattooed the men's Kaena, or the assumed name of a brothel customer, after their real name. These names were inscribed from shoulder to elbow on both arms. This long string of names was followed by the names of her enemies, most likely the spouses of her customers. The name of each of these enemies also had a curse tattooed beside it.

A particularly tough female prostitute by the name of O-Fuji claimed that, "Tattooing on the left and right arms was an old fashioned style," and that she preferred to, "tattoo the names of her male clients in between her fingers."

Illustration on the Following page:
Image of prostitutes bathing. Tattooing can be seen on the upper arms of two of the women. It appears to be writing but is indecipherable.
A Multitude of Hells in the Red Light District 九替十年色地獄 1791
Written by Santo Kyoten 山東京伝 1761-1816
Illustrated by Torii Kyonaga 鳥居清長 1752-1815

In this illustration a courtesan is preparing to have the first joint of her finger cut off in order to prove her love. She is in competition with another courtesan who just tattooed herself to lure the same man. One woman holds a razor while another woman readies a cast iron tea pot. The fellow courtesan on the right will swing the pot onto the top of the razor severing the pinky finger.

From *A Multitude of Hells in the Red Light District* 1790

The whimsical reader *A Collection of This and That* from the first year of Kanei, 1624, contains the following entry,

It is said that from days long past tattooing was popular primarily with young people. Many of them were also involved in other supposed testaments of love like shaving the head and cutting off fingers.

Thus we can see that the tradition of tattooing was well established by 1624. The act of tattooing came to represent a strong bond of love between two people, a kind of promise or guarantee of eternal love. At the time it was called Nyu-bokuro, or adding a mole, in addition to Hori Ire, or digging it in. The oldest record we have describing this is the above mentioned prostitute Sakuya of the Nomaya House of ill repute in the Shinmachi section of Osaka tattooing her favorite clients' names into the front of her shoulder.

The tradition of removing tattoos also accompanied the application of tattoos. Removing these vows of love was called 縁切り En Kiri, cutting connection.

Willem R. van Gulik, in his research study *Irezumi,* highlights the prevalence of tattoo removal in artworks of the time. Bandages on the upper arm indicating a vow of love has been removed. At the time, the only two ways this could be done were by moxibustion or by burning it off with a candle.

Edo Era print by Kunisada, from the series 御用十二手箱ノ内 with a poem about removing a tattoo:

It occurs to me
With the incense burning
To set out a candle
Tattoos also burn
And I can scorch off my small tattoo

Tattooing in Edo Era Literature

Tattooing also featured in Edo Era literature, indicating widespread knowledge of the art. This section will highlight some literature from this period that feature tattooing prominently.

***The Great Mirror of Male Love* 1687** (excerpt)
男色大鏡
Ihara Saikaku 井原西鶴 1642 –1693

Within the pages of *The Great Mirror of Male Love* tells of Kanazawa Naiki and Shimokawa Dannosuke, who confessed their love for a Samurai by the name of Shimamura Tonai. They got tattoos as proof of their devotion.

Excerpt from the chapter titled *Nightingale in the Snow*, translated by Paul Gordon Schalow:

Among the lord's pages were two handsome youths, ages sixteen and seventeen, named Kanazawa Naiki and Shimokawa Dannosuke. They could not bear to see the chief retainer fail in his promise to get the nightingale, so they agreed on a plan. First, they galloped to the Samurai's house on their horses and left their attendants two blocks this side of the place. They then made their way to the inner gate alone, pounded the door open, and leapt noisily onto the bamboo veranda.

"Are you Shimamura Tonai?" They demanded. "Pardon our intrusion but we have come for your life."
Tonai did not understand what they were talking about, but when he looked at them he saw a perfect cherry blossom and a lovely autumn leaf.

"Yes, boys. Death comes but once. let me die defending you. No need to give me the details. Put your minds at ease." He took out three suits of chain mail and unsheathed his long bladed spear.

"Your pursuers should be here at any moment," he warned. "Be on your guard." But neither of the young men made any effort to ready himself. They just grinned at each other. This dampened Tonai's fiery spirit.

"Well now," he said. "Tell me what is going on."
The two boys spoke simultaneously. "It is not at all what you think. We are here to take your life. Then everything in the house will be ours to do with as we please."

"I suppose you are after the birds, too," he replied. "A moment ago I promised to die defending you. I guess I no longer have anything to lose. Here, take them." He handed them two nightingales in a round cage fringed with multicolored tassels.
The boys thanked him and left.

At the gate, they summoned their attendants and instructed them to leave a large chest with Tonai. They then returned to Sakurada. Thus, the problem of the nightingale was successfully resolved.

That night, Dannosuke and Naiki went again in secret to the Samurai's house to properly express their thanks for his help that day. "We feel that this little episode was fate's way of allowing us to get to know you. Although you undoubtedly find us unappealing, we would like to ask you to be our lover and teach us the way of love."

"Normally, I should make the advances," he replied. "Your request is kind, but I am not worthy of it and cannot accept. For one, I would have a hard time choosing between the two of you, and besides, I have no way of knowing how sincere your love for me really is."

Naiki and Dannosuke's faces flushed with anger. "As proof of the depth of our love..." they began, and together bared their shoulders. On his left arm Dannosuke had tattooed the name Shimamura, and on Naiki's arm was the name Tonai.

"We did this in good faith even before consummating our love with you," they said.

"That is something women do," the Samurai scoffed. "I will not make a vow of this sort unless I am convinced first that you are willing to die like men for my sake."

"Do you think that we are the type who would hesitate to give our lives for you? Give us that chest," they said. They immediately threw it open, and inside were two low tables and a pair of small short swords wrapped in paper, placed there in preparation for committing seppuku.

Tonai was shocked. He jumped between them and asked for an explanation.

"This," they said, "was just in case we had failed earlier to get the nightingale. We would not have returned home alive. If we were willing to die manfully for the sake of a bird, don't you think we would be all the more willing to give our lives for you?" They were weeping.

At this, Tonai relented and made profuse apologies to the boys. "From now on, you will be the only ones I love." So saying, he bit off the last joint of each of his little fingers and gave one to each of the young men. In this way their destinies were joined.

Excerpt from:
The Great Mirror of Male Love
by Ihara Saikaku
Translated by Paul Gordon Schalow.
1990
Stanford University Press

Romantic Embroilments Born in Edo
(summary & selected dialogue)
江戸生艶気樺焼
1787
Kyoden Santo 1761 – 1816

This is the story of a boy named Enjiro, who is about to turn 20 and become an adult. He is the only son and the family is fabulously wealthy but he seeks only to become a Casanova.

In this scene Enjiro is lounging and reading a book whilst smoking a Kiseru pipe. He laments being born the way he was,

Why did I have to come into the world in this body? Such a bore. Why couldn't I have been born on a less auspicious day?

In this next scene Enjiro pays a visit to the son of a local Doraku 道楽, a person who excels at debauchery. The son, Kitari Kinosuke states,

Finally we can start on our plan to make you a lover. The first thing we need to do is make you LOOK like a player.

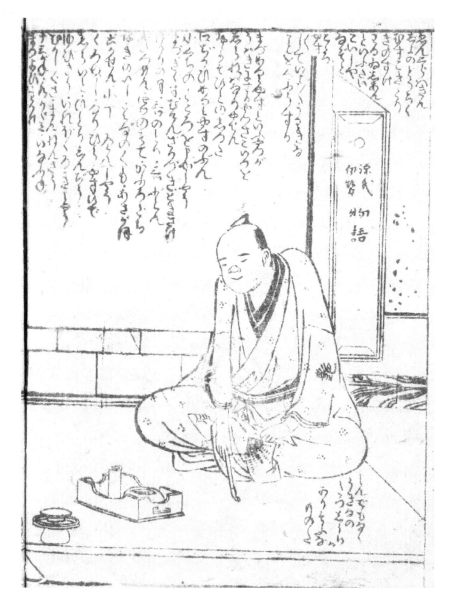

He goes on to inform Enjiro that,
The first step in looking like a great romantic is getting tattooed.

In this scene he is listing the colorful names of the women he is supposed to have dated and whose names he will tattoo on his arm.

Summer moon, Lingering Heat, Two Letters, My Heart...

In this scene Enjiro gets himself tattooed with the names of 20 or 30 women across both arms and even in between his fingers. He rejoices, *Through this pain I will achieve my dream!*

He is advised that, *If you have broken up with a girl you should get her name erased. It's bad luck to leave it there so after breaking up, get it burned off.*

Enjiro comments,

It's certainly painful to become a great lover.

Over the course of the story Enjiro spends money hand over fist hiring women to pretend to be madly in love with him, commissioning tales of his romantic exploits and begging his parents to disown him due to his "debauchery."

In the climax of the story (shown above and on the following page) he has hired a courtesan to elope and commit suicide with him as a pair of star crossed lovers.

He has already arranged for another set of accomplices to "stop" the suicide. In this scene Enjiro is "in disguise" and is "eloping" with his lover. The other workers at this house of ill repute see him off shouting,

Take your time while you escape!

Unfortunately, at the scene of their dual suicide a pair of thieves presents themselves and declare,

If we are caught, we are dead men, so killing you is our only option!

Enjiro begs their mercy and the robbers decide to simply relieve them of their rich belongings.

Enjiro,

Please, this is not what it seems!

Courtesan,

What on earth is going on?!

The pair, deprived of all their possessions, save an umbrella (and strangely his Katana, which may have been hard to pawn) make their way back to town. (Enjiro's tattoos are visible scrawled down his left arm.)

In the end, due to these exploits, Enjiro becomes a "famous lover" with this tale being told all over Edo.

The Mission of the Tattooed Arm (excerpt)
腕雕一心命
By Shikitei Sanba 式亭三馬 1776 - 1822
Illustrations by Utagawa Kunimitsu 歌川国満 ? - ?

In this story four Otokodate, or street knights, decide they must get tattooed by the finest artists in Edo. After getting the work done they go out drinking to celebrate. That night the tattoos come alive and separating from their bodies. The tattoos are all historical figures who go back to the actions they did before they died.

These four men got the greatest tattoos in Japan, therefore they felt they were at the peak of their adventure. The men completely bonded with their tattoos. However, skillful works like these have mysterious powers. As they slept soundly that night, the four men's tattoos began to move and pull away from their hosts and flit and float about in the sky.

Later, the tattoos separated from the bodies of the four Otokodate, so floating in the air there was a devil, Samurai and the severed head of a man and a woman. The floating tattoos called out to one another.

The story continues with each of the tattoos going off on their own adventure. Two of the tattoos, are Namakubi, or severed heads. The one on the left is of a semi-legendary figure named Inokuma who was executed due to an affair with the wife of a noble, who is the head on the right.

The head of Inokuma and the woman with a scroll in her mouth stayed out so late they were unable to crawl back into their body. They came to the somewhat questionable decision to continue their travels.

Woman's severed head :
Inukuma! Would you hurry up! Fly up over here

Inukuma :
You know if we are seen in the daytime flying around like this people will think we are kites! By the way, that piece of paper you got in your mouth is nothing! I have this big heavy chunk of armor. Its liable to break my teeth! What terrible luck!

Some of the other tattoos actually switch owners and hilarity ensues…

| One of the men got the scene of the 11th century Samurai Watanabe no Tsuna fighting a demon at Rashomon gate tattooed on his back. | Another member of the gang got a tattoo of the 12th century Samurai Fujiwara Kagekiyo grabbing the Shikoro (neck guard-flap) on the back of Juro Mihonoya's helmet during the Genpei War. |

In this scene everyone is amazed that the tattoos have switched bodies. The demon is grabbing the helmet of Mihonoya and Kagekiyo is grabbing Watanabe. One man places the blame on the skill of the artist:

You know, we got a famous artist of create the designs and we had renowned engraver do the tattooing, it should be no surprise that they poured their souls into their work. Those should must have somehow pulled free. I've never heard of anything like this.

隼人・熊襲
Hayato · Kumaso

蝦夷・琉球
Emishi · Ryukyu

Hayato and Kumaso

Many of the early 20th century researchers into tattooing in Japan describe a re-emergence of tattooing in the 1600's after a lapse of a 1000 years and puzzle over the source. The peaceful era that followed the warring states period of 1467-1600 and the subsequent shift from a nation continuously at war to a unified country allowed people to notice such things.

Researchers such as Tanaka Kogai and Ema Tsutomu have theorized the re-emergence of tattooing among the mainland Japanese was due to the absorbing of the Ryukyu Islands, the Ainu or both. However, the Satsuma region in the southern Kyushu island is where the Hayato and Kumaso peoples lived. It is possible that the tattooing tradition seen in the soldiers from Satsuma is a holdover from the traditions of those two ancient tribes.

The Hayato 隼人, or "falcon people," and the Kumaso 熊襲, or "attacking bear" people were two (or possibly more) cultures that remained separate from the Yamato in central Japan and the Emishi and Ainu peoples in northeastern Japan. The Kumaso may actually consist of two different groups, the Kuma and the So, both of which lived in the same region. They were both conquered and absorbed into Japanese culture, though the Hayato culture seems to have remained independent longer.

The Hayato also seemed to have held a higher status because after their subjugation they were managed by a government official known as the *Hayato-shi* 隼人司.

While the Kumaso are mentioned in the more legendary portions of the Chronicles of Japan, the Hayato are recorded in various historical texts as late as the beginning of the Heian Era 710-794.

-Takemitsu, Makoto (1999). *Encyclopedia of the Kojiki and Nihon Shoki.*

The Hayato were forced off their lands and brought to an area south of Kyoto. There they worked as guards, bamboo artisans and Sumo wrestlers. Below is a picture of a Haniwa 埴輪 (clay figurine) depicting a person in a wrestling pose from the 3rd~6th century CE. The figure, which is 113 cm tall and found in Wakayama City, wears a Fundoshi (loin cloth) and has traces of crimson paint on the face. The painting, which is on both sides of the nose and under the eyes, could be decorative paint but could also indicate tattooing on the face.

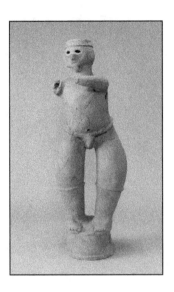

The Japanese Sumo Federation states that,

The earliest examples of Sumo appear in The Kojiki (712) and The Nihon Shoki (720) and from then on were a part of harvest ceremonies and other annual events. Sumo was also practiced by Samurai up through the end of the Warring States Period in 1600 as part of their training.... In the peaceful 17th century that followed Sumo as tests of strength became popular and eventually solidified into a business. Different Beya, or Sumo training houses, were founded and regular events were held.

In the Early Edo Era, however, the competitors seemed to have been people that liked to test their strength against each other in competitions known as Yori-Zumo (spontaneous Sumo.) Many of these men tattooed themselves (This will be discussed later in the Otokodate and Sumo Chapter.) However, it seems by the 1800's, formal Sumo wrestlers (those employed by/living full time at a Beya) were not tattooed. This may have been due to a government mandate, but that is unclear. Below are some illustrations of Sumo wrestlers from *Illustrations of Sumo Techniques* 相撲取組図 by Kensai Uchizakura 見斎打楼 from 1827. The judges are dressed formally and the event is clearly organized and not Yori-Zumo.

As the illustration on page 71 shows, the area under the Emperor's influence began to expand north and east into the area controlled by the Emishi, and south into the Hayato and Kumaso areas. These cultures in the southern area were probably the original Wajin described in the Chinese texts from the first three centuries CE, however they gradually adopted Japanese customs. The traditions of tattooing disappeared and even the marginally official Keikei 黥刑, tattoo punishment, was abolished. However, as the story of the 500 Samurai from the Satsuma Domain shows, the tradition of tattooing in the Kyushu region continued quite some time after both the Hayato and the Kumaso had been absorbed into Japanese society.

It is not clear how the Hayato and Kumaso culture affected tattooing in Japan, however there are some interesting animal figures carved into stones around the burial site of the son of Emperor Shomu 聖武天皇 701-75. His son, who died at the age of 2 in 728, was buried in Nahoyama Crypt 那富山墓 in Nara City. These simple carvings, known as Hayato Stones, could also be examples of tattoos used by these people.

A Small Record of Old Curios 好古小録 1795.
By Toh Teikan 藤貞幹 1732-1797

The figures were positioned around the area thought to be the tomb of the son of Emperor Shomu. The figure on the right has North written above it. Traditionally this is the rat but due to the fact it is positioned to the northwest, dog would be most appropriate.

Chinese Zodiac

The other Hayato stones are positioned northeast, southeast and southwest and therefore they should be a dog (or boar), Ox (or tiger), Dragon (or snake) and Sheep (or monkey). The fourth image was uncovered in the Edo Era.

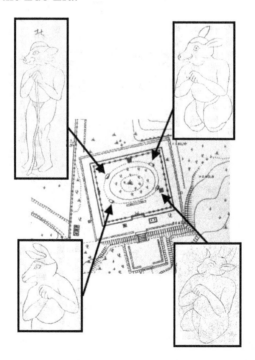

Position of the Hayato Stones at Nahoyama Crypt

Ainu Tattooing Traditions

Emishi paying homage to Prince Shotoku. Produced in 1324, based on Shotokutaishi e-den e-maki, made in 1069.

Some researchers consider the Emishi 蝦夷 and the Ainu アイヌ to be the same culture, but others think they are separate. They are a group (or groups) that lived in the northern part of the main island of Japan, Honshu.

The first mention of Eimishi in literature dates to AD 400, in which they are mentioned as "the hairy people" from the Chinese records. Some Emishi tribes resisted the rule of the Japanese during the Late Nara and Early Heian periods (7th-10th centuries AD). The origin of the Emishi is unknown, but they are often thought to have descended from the Jomon People and been related to the Ainu. -Wikipedia.

The cultures that were originally in Japan but were forced northward following a new migration from southern Korea and costal China are:

Emishi 蝦夷
Ebisu　恵比寿
Ainu アイヌ
Ezo　蝦夷

The Ebisu/ Emishi were initially successful in fending off the Yamato Japanese due to their hit and run style of horseback archery. These tactics were successful against the larger Japanese units. Eventually the Japanese began to adopt the Emishi tactics and began to take over their lands, eventually either bringing them under Japanese rule or driving most of the Emishi into Hokkaido.

The success of the gradual change in battle tactics came at the very end of the 8th century in the 790s under the command of the general Sakanoue no Tamuramaro. They either submitted themselves to imperial authority or migrated further north, some to Hokkaido. By the mid-9th century, most of their land in Honshu was conquered, and they ceased to be independent. However, they continued to be influential in local politics as subjugated, though powerful, Emishi families created semi-autonomous feudal domains in the north. In the two centuries following the conquest, a few of these domains became regional states that came into conflict with the central government.

- Farris, William Wayne, *Heavenly Warriors* (Cambridge: Harvard University Press1992)

Sakhalin Ainu

Kuril Islands
Ainu

Hokkaido Ainu

Tohoku Ainu

Historical Accounts of Ainu Tattooing

In the Ainu language tattooing is known as Shinue or Shinui, though there are regions that use the word Kesho. Shinue means "to dye" while Kesho, is the Japanese word meaning cosmetics and is used in the same way as the inland population. The tradition of tattooing seems to have lasted amongst the Ainu at least until the mid-1930's.

The earliest record of Ainu tattooing was by the Italian named Girolamo de Angelis who, in 1621, described the women in Hokkaido as having tattooing on their hands and around their mouths. The first Japanese record of Ainu tattooing was in the 1680s, and recorded women having tattooing around the mouth.

Hirai Masagoro 1863-1913 went to Hokkaido several times between 1886 and 1888 and met with many Ainu people living in various regions. By that time the Ainu had been made Japanese citizens and given family registers along with a Japanese surname. Most of the people he interviewed were able to speak Japanese but still maintained Ainu traditions. In Hirai's survey he states that there were over 17,000 Ainu in Hokkaido at the time. He discussed his findings in the *Tokyo Humanities Society Magazine* 東京人類学会雑誌 a series of articles from September of 1888 to August of 1893.

September 1888

Hirai asked several different groups of Ainu about their origins and why they came to Hokkaido. He collected multiple versions however most stated they were forced out of Shamochi (the Ainu word for the Japanese mainland) by the Shamo (the Japanese.) When they arrived on "this island" (Hokkaido) they found a tribe of people already living here.

Interview with a woman named Kawamura Kiku from the Shiribeshi no Kuni 後志国 in south western Hokkaido.

I don't know much about when we came here because it was generations ago whoever there was a different race from the Ainu already on the island. Since they liked to hide under the leaves of Koro or butterbur plant we called them Koropok-guru コロポック ル the people under the butterbur. They were a lot shorter than us and lived in 竪穴 pit-houses, which were partially dug into the earth. They were good at making earthenware bowls and would sometimes trade with us for food. However, they would only stick their arm in the window and never show their faces. One time an Ainu person pulled the arm of a Koropok-guru through the window into the house. They got mad at this and left. Anytime you find the remains of a pit-house with pottery, small knives or metal bowls, it was probably a Koropok-guru house.

Interview with an Ainu named Tamura Monsuke of Akkeshigun 厚岸郡釧路国（くしろのくに）

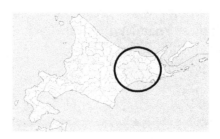

The Koropok-guru were only about 8 Sun, 24 cm, tall. One Ainu girl became friendly with a female Koropok-guru and traded food. However, the Koropoku-guru girl always kept the sleeve of

her shirt over her face even when she was trading goods she kept one hand over her face. One day a man pulled her hand away and everyone could see she had tattooing around her mouth. At this time the Ainu had no tradition of tattooing, so everyone was very curious and they asked,

"Why do you do this tattooing?"

The answer was,

"when boys and girls are young we can't tell the difference between them, so we mark the girls by tattooing them."

Since the Ainu also had a tradition of shaving the heads of children, they also couldn't tell the difference between young boys and girls so they copied the Koropok-guru and began the tradition of tattooing.

Another tale from the same area:

There are a lot of pit-dwellings in this area and most people believe these are the remains of Koropok-guru villages. They would also come and trade for food, but would only put their hand in the window, therefore hiding their bodies. One day an Ainu pulled a Koropok-guru into the house by their hand and everyone saw the tattooing on the arm and around the mouth of a beautiful girl. The Koropok-guru became angry at this and moved away. The Ainu women, after seeing the beautiful tattooing on the Koropok-guru girl, began to tattoo themselves.

Interestingly Tamabayashi records a tale that is virtually the opposite of the above tale.

The Ainu fought a war with the Koropok-guru and won. The women they kept as prisoners kept trying to escape so the Ainu tattoed them so that they would look like Ainu women.

In the August 1892 issue, Hirai talks of his research trip to Sapporo, the present day capital of Hokkaido. There he interviewed a woman about her experience getting tattooed. She (name unknown) and her husband named Charisangu ran an Ainu restaurant. Hirai indicates the woman was only partially fluent in Japanese and recorded the sections of her story that he could understand.

I started Nue, tattooing, when I was a young girl...it really hurt...I was crying and thought I would die...it was as if I was going to die (she held her hand to her chest) I couldn't stand it...they splashed water on me to wake me up....they cut me...I wanted others to know my pain... I wanted others to see...how much it hurt. If the tattooist was good your mouth would heal in 3 days and your hands in 4 days. If the person was clumsy you could have swelling for a long time.

-Hirai Masagoro *Tokyo Humanities Society Magazine1888-93*

Over the course of Hirai's interviews he found most villages only had one or two tattooists but there was no guild or formal training. Those that thought they could do it made themselves available.

The researcher Michioka Shinichi witnessed firsthand the tattooing traditions in Hokkaido during his trips to the region in the late 1920s and early 1930s and described it as follows,

Even these days women of the Ainu tribe tattoo themselves around the mouth and on the back of the hands. The tradition of tattooing the backs of the hands, fingers and arms still remains with the women of the Ryukyu Islands (Okinawa), *who share an ancestor with the Ainu. The designs used for the tattoos in Ryukyu islands varies with the island, but all tend to do it on both the left and right hands as well as the arms. It tends to not be done on other parts of the body. Tattooing is typically done just before marriage thought it can be done afterward. For them it was considered to be exactly that same as the everyday cosmetics applied by women living on the main island of Japan. It would probably best be described as a natural step forward in women's beautification.*

Though the sight of a girl with tattoos around the mouth resembling the facial hair of boys is shocking to those living in the central island of Japan, young people brought up with such a tradition extending long into the past find it beautiful to their own eyes. Further, they even desire such tattoos to be a degree darker and thereby appear more fresh and vibrant.

- Michioka Shinichi *In the Footsteps of the Ainu* 1934

He also records and rejects one of the theories regarding the origins of the tattooing tradition,

There are also the tales of the Ainu of Karafuto, the Japanese name for the Russian Sakhalin Islands, abducting Ainu women of Hokkaido and tattooing them in order to make them repulsive to their own people that do not really seem plausible in my opinion. The tattooing I have researched does not seem to reflect that story.

-Michioka Shinich *In the Footsteps of the Ainu* 1934

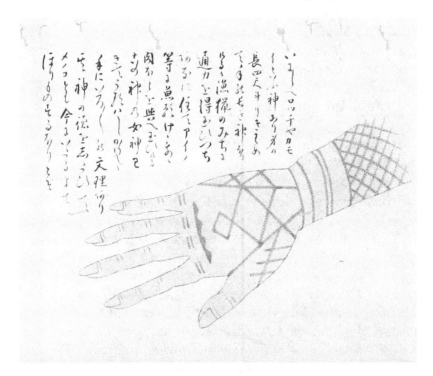

Illustration: Tattoo pattern from the Edo Era book *Unusual Scenes from Ezo Island*. This example shows the back of a woman's hand and forearm. The forearm has a Uroko, or fish scale pattern. The meaning of the design on the back of the hand is unclear.

Tamabayashi also recorded a completely different origin to Ainu tattooing.

There is a legend regarding the origin of Ainu women tattooing themselves. Long ago the god Aioina and his sister, who was a goddess, descended from the heavens. Aioina taught the Ainu many things. His sister, who was tattooed, taught the Ainu women the art of tattooing. The reason was if a devil or demon came it would see the tattooing and think that the Ainu woman was a god and then flee. Therefore Ainu women believe that tattooing themselves will protect themselves from evil demons. The goddess included a warning with her teachings. She told them it would be a great crime if a woman marries without getting a tattoo. They would plunge into the depths of hell.

Ainu Tattoo Ink and Tattooing Method

Hirai records the making of the tattoo ink and application of the tattoo as follows:

First scrape and clean the bottom of a cauldron. Fill it with water and bring the water to a boil over the Irori 圍爐裡 shallow fire pit inside the house. Throw in several strips of the Aodamo Ash tree, called Iwa by the Ainu. The bark of this tree produces an indigo color. Add several paper thin strips of birch bark on top of the fire. This will cause oily smoke to start coating the bottom of the cauldron. The strips of Iwa in the pot will gradually cause the water to become darker indigo in color. The tattooist would rub the bottom of the cauldron with their finger and mark the areas on the receiver's body. This may include drawing a design. Then they would use either a razor or Makri to make scratch like marks. When blood begins to well up, a rag dipped in the astringent indigo water would be used to clean the area. Ash from the bottom of the cauldron called Nabe-sumi, or pot ink, would be rubbed into the area repeatedly. This is the tattooing process. As the woman from the Ainu restaurant in Sapporo mentioned, if a girl passes out during the process, they will dump water on her to revive them before proceeding.

Shinichi as well as Tamabayashi also record slightly different procedures:

Birch bark is burned in a fire and the smoke collects on the bottom of a pot resulting in Nabe-sumi, or pot ink. This is flaked off and boiled in a pot with cloth that has been dyed with indigo resulting in a dark indigo color. This mixture is boiled down until it reaches the desired consistency.

- Michioka Shinichi *In the Footsteps of the Ainu* 1934

After cutting with the Makiri knife, Nabe-sumi is rubbed in. After that a rag is soaked in the juice wrung from butterbur leaves, or in some areas grape leaves, and is used to blot the cut periodically as it heals in order to increase the color.

-Tamabayashi Haruo *The Hundred Shapes of Tattoos 1956*

Examples of Ainu Hand Tattoos

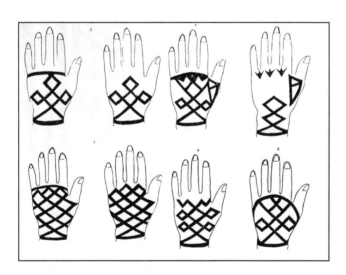

Tattooing variations on the backs of women's hands.

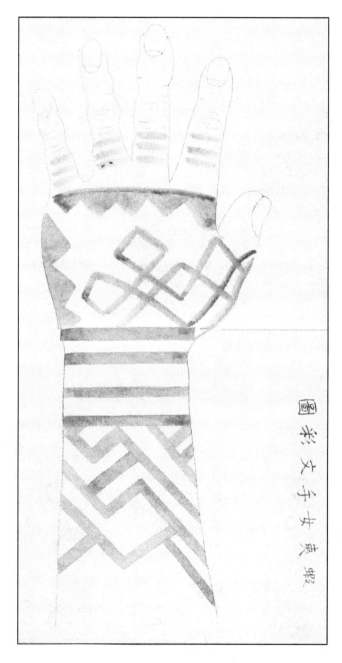

Detail of an Ainu girl's tattooed hand from *An Emissary's Log of Ezo*使鰕夷行記 Author unknown. Edo Era.

Tattooing by Men

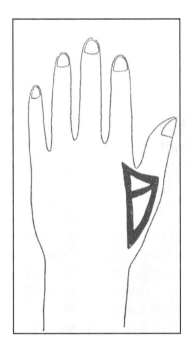

Hirai mentions he saw men with tattoos. He records that Ainu people told him,

Long ago men also used to have tattoos, but nowadays it is only common to have one. Typically this is an X tattooed between the thumb and index finger of the left hand.

Another common tattoo is a ▼ this symbol, which could represent the circus toy called a Ryugo 輪鼓, which is a kind of Chinese yoyo. It is also used as a clan mark, a military signal flag and a horse walking pattern. The illustration of an Ainu man's tattoo is from a 1939 study by Jidama and Itoh.

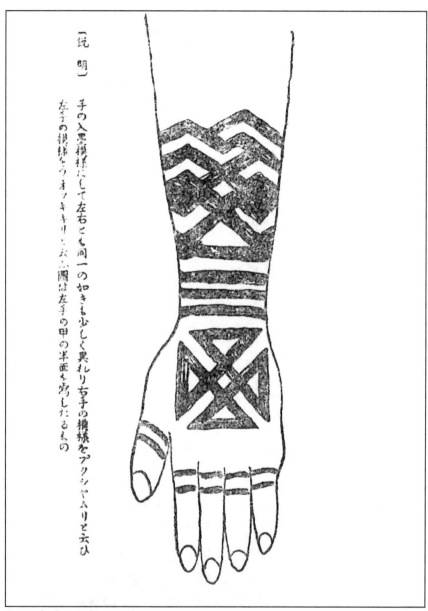

〔説明〕手の入墨模様にして左右とも同一の如きも少しく異れり右手の模様をピクシヤムリと云ひ左手の模様をウオツキキリと云ふ図は左手の甲の半面を写したるもの

Translation of Notation:

The tattooing on both the right and left hands looks similar but it differs somewhat. The tattoo design on the right hand is called Pikushamuri. The tattoo design on the left hand is called Uokki Kiri. The illustration is a reproduction of the back of the left hand.
Michioka Shinich's *In the Footsteps of the Ainu* 1934.

An Ainu girl with eyebrow, mouth and hand tattoos from *An Emissary's Log of Ezo* 使鰕夷行記 Author unknown. Edo Era.

Tattooing around the Mouth

Both Hirai and Michioka wrote similar accounts of the stages of tattooing around the mouth. Michioka's report had detailed illustrations so this description is primarily based on his report.

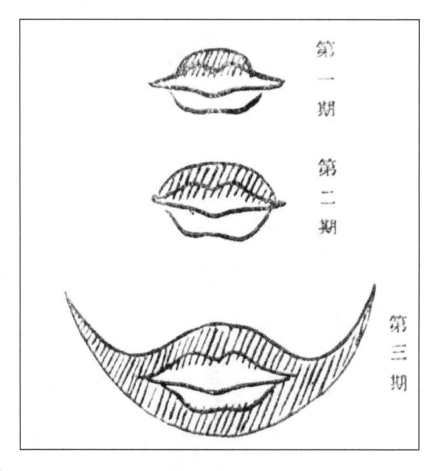

Illustration of the three stages of Ainu tattooing. Michioka Shinich's *In the Footsteps of the Ainu* 1934.

The tattoo is done with a sharp implement to make many small incision above the upper lip. Then the indigo/cinder dye is rubbed into the cuts. For a time, the entire upper lip swells and for a few days it is impossible for her to eat. After a week it had fully healed and the fresh marking left behind by the tattoo will be very beautiful.

The second period is around the time the girl becomes fourteen or fifteen years old, whereupon the tattooed area is expanded. By the end of this period the tattooing has proceeded considerably.

The third tattooing period comes when the girl is around eighteen or nineteen years of age, coinciding with the time girls would be getting married. It goes without saying that not completing this tattooing would be a shame for the person and, at the same time, a lot of the girls seek to have the full tattooing done as soon as possible in order to complete this beautification ritual and thereby become more appealing. There are even said to be cases where the girl does not wait for her parents to order her to get it done but rather seeks out a capable person within the village to complete the tattooing for her.

Additional tattooing such as connecting the two eyebrows and applying a certain design extending from the back of the hand to the forearm were done at a later time and not subject to any particular timeline. Traditionally tattoos look very fresh and intense at the beginning but their beauty tends to fade as the months and years pass and the effect dims somewhat. When the brightness of the tattoo begins to fade it begins to look unappealing.

For a period of several years following a girl's final tattooing at eighteen or nineteen, the newness of the tattooing holds but it eventually begins to fade. Thus in order for a girl to retain her visual vitality she would have to do follow up surgery in order to restore the tattoo to its original freshness.

The women currently living in the Shiraoi region, who are around forty years of age never went past the first stage of tattooing surgery. The fact that these women have not done the surgery widening the area of tattooing is likely due to the fact that twenty-seven or twenty-eight years ago they came to terms with the fact that the arguments for conducting this surgery were just not sufficient. An Ainu woman that had this tattooing talked about her feelings regarding it.

I know this tradition has been handed down to us from the past, but why such a stupid thing would be done is beyond me. Nowadays, no matter how much girls are encouraged to do it, none get tattoos. When I was a child, I saw others having it done so I just accepted it as something that had to happen. The fact of the matter, the reality is that is really hurts. Nowadays when we interact with the Shishamu, the Ainu word referring to mainland Japanese people, it is embarrassing and I cast about for some method to have it removed. I've spoken to several doctors and some of them have tried to burn it off with chemicals but my tattooing cannot be removed. I am deeply troubled by this.

This confession was done in order that the youth of today are not deceived by anyone.

Illustration from *Dictionary of Ezo* 蝦夷品彙訳言 Yuki San 結城 粲 Printed in 嘉永 7 1854. The text reads,

This illustration is from Karafuto Island. As you can see in the picture the woman has extensive tattooing around her lips. Her hair is cut short. She is wearing a skirt made of seal skin.

Illustration from *Dictionary of Ezo* 蝦夷品彙訳言 Yuki San 結城
粲 Printed in 嘉永 7 1854.

The text surrounding the couple reads,

*This is from Edoropu (Etorofu)Island.   The man's name is
Ahino and the woman's name is Shime no ko.*

*As the illustration shows, the woman has tattooing around her
lips and has rings in her ears.   This indicates she has a man (a
husband.)*

Tattooing between the Eyebrows

The tradition of tattooing the space between one eyebrow and the other is done in Shiraoi and areas west of that. It is not done in the Hidaka area. There is a tale from amongst those that do tattooing, though it can differ according to the area. In the Horobetsu region it is said that if a young married girl does not get tattooed and happens to die, then in her next life she will be born as Karasu, a crow. In the Shiraoi region it is said that if a woman who is not tattooed dies, the gods will be angered so, a piece of bamboo should be taken up and they should be tattooed. For this reason, there is a tradition of, before burial, tattooing the area around the mouth on any girl who should die without having the surgery done.

Originally tattooing was done with arrowheads, but later the Ainu began trading for small iron pocket knives from the Japanese mainlanders.

Tattooed woman and husband from *Unusual Scenes from Ezo Island* 蝦夷島之奇観 This book is undated but by Hata Awagimaru 秦檍丸 1764-1808.

Tattooing on the Cheeks

Ainu cheek tattoos are somewhat lesser well known. In his 1786 book *Notes on Eastern Travels* 東遊雑記 Furukawa Koshokan wrote,

They often have plum or chrysanthemum flower tattooed onto their cheek. The handiwork is quite good. The area around the lips is also tattooed with a pale blue. The tattooing is surprisingly well done. In this area the women do not have any tattooing on their hands. I think from this we can conclude that tattooing by Emishi people varies by region.

Illustration from Record of Ezo 蝦夷記. Edo Period. The text reads,
This is how women from the upper classes look. All such women have wildflower or a broken latticework tattooing on their face (connecting the eyebrows.) There is also light tattooing around the lips which makes them appear to be bluish.

97

Tattooing as Treatment

There is some evidence that the Ainu used tattooing as treatment for injuries or disease. The illustration below shows a tattoo of a Manji 卍 with lines extending outward. This tattoo, which was on the shoulder of a woman, from Matsuno's 1958 study of Ainu traditions 十勝アイヌ文身の研究 was described as "treatment for a persistent injury." On the shoulder of a woman. Terada Seiichi also notes that,

Tattooing is used as treatment of illness or injury amongst the Ainu. Tattooing was used as a remedy when traditional medicines proved ineffective. This is similar to the tradition of using tattoos to treat rheumatism, pain in the joints, bruises and stubborn old injuries in Morocco and Algeria.

There does not seem to have been any influence from Ainu tattooing on mainland Japanese tattooing but as the use of Kanji tattoos for medical treatment, the reverse seems to be true.

Tattooing in the Ryukyu Islands

Illustration of the Ryukyu Islands, now called Okinawa from the 1702 Encyclopedia 和漢三才図絵.

Tattooing is called Hazuki針衝, or striking with a needle, in the Ryukyu islands. The earliest mention of tattooing in the Ryukyu Islands, now called Okinawa, can be found in the *Tales of Ryukyu* section of a Chinese history *The Book of Sui*:

Married women take ink and tattoo their hands with images of snakes and insects.

Since this is markedly different from the tattooing recorded in later works, it is possible *The Book of Sui* was referring to Taiwan.

The designs used for the tattoos in Ryukyu islands vary island by island, however there are some consistent features. The tattooing tends to be on both hands and extend up the forearm. The tattooing is done almost exclusively by women and not done on any other parts of the body. Tattooing is typically done just before marriage though it can be done afterward.

The amount of tattooing a girl has depends on whether or not she is married as well as her social status. Unmarried girls will have relatively simple tattoos, but after getting married more extensive tattooing will be done. In other words, half of the tattoo will be done at one house and the other half at the new house.

In the Ming Dynasty of China Jo Hoko mentions tattooing in *The Record of Chusan* (Chusan is the Chinese name for the Ryukyu Islands.)

Girls from the age of fifteen use a needle to stab ink into the backs of their hands.

In the pages of *Essays On the Edge of the Eastern Sea* by court official of the Ryukyu Kingdom by the name of Kishaba Choken 喜舍場 朝賢 (1840-1916) writes,

When girls are engaged to be married they tattoo the outside of their fingers. In addition, there are no people over the age of twenty-one without tattooing. Any over that age without tattoos would be ridiculed. There are women with cherry blossoms tattooed in black. This is an old style that meant a woman was of high birth.

As the years pass the Sumi (ink) fades. The tattooing is redone to make it fresh again. People will get tattooed five or six times, so as not to end their lives with inferior faded tattoos.

Now, with the establishment of Prefectures (instead of the Edo Era domains) tattooing has been ruled illegal. If you are caught tattooing you will be arrested and thrown in jail. In the end it has become a crime.

The first time a girl is tattooed, a quiet house is prepared. Close relatives are invited and a feast is held at the retreat. At this time girls that are 12 or 13 are tattooed as shown in the illustration below.

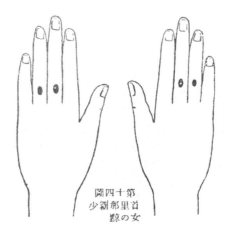

If any girl that is married and does not have tattooing should die, they will surely go to the other side. There they will have to pull a troublesome root from the ground. This is considered to be the most difficult work and you will be condemned to do it for all time.

In his 1894 book, Exploration of the Southern Islands 南島探驗 the anthropologist Sasamori Gisuke 笹森儀助 (1845-1915) investigated the meaning of Ryukyu tattoo symbols.

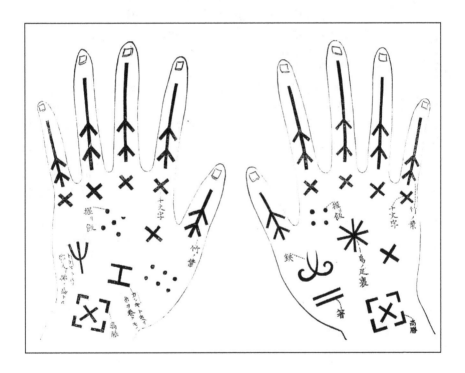

Tattoo	Meaning
+	This cross shape represents a woven pattern. This tattoo is done to represent "skillfully" weaving.
● ● ● ● ● ●	These six "stars" represent the Kashiki, a Ryukyu spindle. The Kashiki, and the implied thread wrapped around it, performs a similar function to the cross shape. A four "star" version represents the same thing.
I	This symbol also represents the Kashiki, a Ryukyu symbol. This is possibly the view from the side while the "six stars" are the view from the top.
═	These represent Hashi, or chopsticks. A desire for food to be abundant.
[X]	This symbol represents a high class meal with delicious food. For centuries the Ryukyu islands had a complicated caste system. Generally speaking Churyu, or middle class, and above had a tradition of eating fine food. By tattooing this symbol on their hands women expressed their desire to move up in rank.
● ● ● ● ●	This symbol is Nigiri Meishi also known as Onigiri, or rice balls. This also represents a desire or prayer to have the same amount of food as the higher classes. In addition, being in a higher class would mean no shortage of food.

Tattoo	Meaning
	  These two marks represent the footprint of a bird, but the meaning is unclear.
 Bamboo grass	
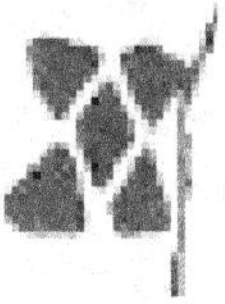	A shape that represents the traditional clothing. This symbol appears in the following illustrations
	This is a tattoo of scissors. These represent a prayer to become skillful at weaving.
	This is a mark tattooed to banish Tokeya, an evil spirit.

Sasamori also notes that,

Older women will have the tattoos extending all the way up to the elbow. With this you can tell at a glance who is a skilled weaver.

The tattooing is done from around the ages of 11-13. This also corresponds to the time boys come of age.

Bamboo leaves grow straight, just as bamboo does. It is said this is what you should model your spirit after.

Yoshihara Shigeie included the following two illustrations in the June 1900 edition of the Tokyo Anthropological Society Magazine 東京人類学会雑誌. They are the right and left hands of a woman on the main island of Okinawa. Unfortunately, he doesn't include any information regarding the meanings of the tattoos.

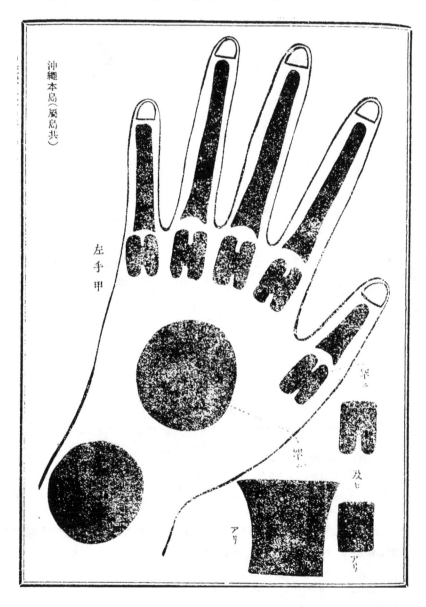

These tattoos seem to cover the tops of the fingers and a large portion of the back of the hand. While the tattoos introduced by Sasamori seem to be a collection of talismans and badges of merit, the ones recorded by Yoshihara simply color the backs of the fingers and sections of the back of the palm and wrist.

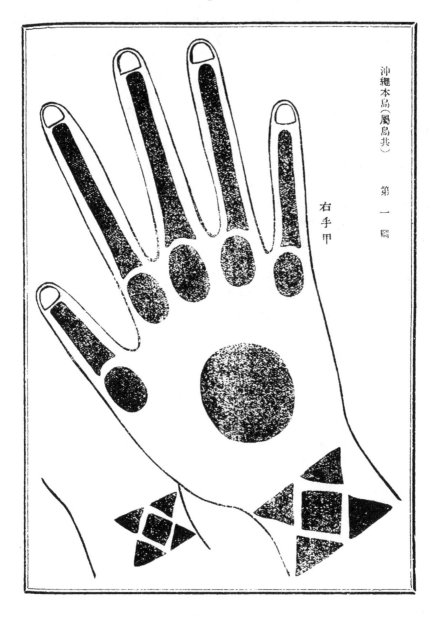

The Japanese government banned tattooing in Okinawa in 1899. An article by the Ryukyu News Agency stated that "tattooing is to be considered a crime...." And that "Anyone doing tattooing is in violation of code 428 section 9 and anyone caught will face one day in jail and a fine of ten Sen to one Yen."

This did not completely eliminate the tradition as even post world war two researchers were able to interview women who had traditional hand tattooing. This means the tattooing tradition lasted for over 1200 years in the Ryukyu/ Okinawan islands.

It is not clear if Ainu or Ryukyu tattooing had any influence on the re-emergence and subsequent popularity of tattooing amongst certain classes. Some Japanese researchers such as Tanaka Kogai and Ema Tsutomu have theorized the re-emergence of tattooing among the mainland Japanese was due to contact with either the Ryukyu islanders or the Ainu or both.

At any rate the traditions of Ainu and Ryukyu tattooing seem to have developed independently of each other. This would imply that there are at least six tattooing traditions in Japan.

- Pre-historic (Jomon Era)
- Ainu
- Ryukyu
- Buddhist priests
- Satsuma (possibly a holdover from Hayato / Kumaso traditions)
- Mainland tattooing (beginning in the Edo Era)

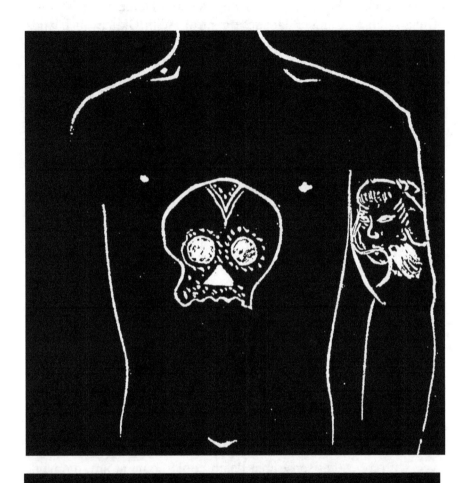

The Spread of Tattooing

In the fourteenth year of Keicho (1609) the Shimatsu Clan led an effort to subjugate the Ryukyu Islands, now known as Okinawa. In the sixteenth year of Keicho (1611) they succeeded and the Ryukyu Islands became part of the Satsuma Domain and thereby officially coming under Japanese control. With Okinawan Islands now part of Japan some researchers feel knowledge of Ryukyu traditions spread with its integration into Japan.

Tanaka believes the Ryukyu tradition of tattooing was influential in the re-emergence of tattooing in the Edo era.

In all likelihood the custom amongst both the society of women working in the brothels and young homosexual men of tattooing a vow of love on the body was inspired by this Ryukyu tradition. In other words the tradition of the Ryukyu women and girls tattooing the name of their fiancé or post marriage tattooing of their partner's name as a symbol of marriage was taken up by the prostitutes of our county to display sincerity and true feelings. It was the Ryukyu traditions that gave rise to the practice of tattooing men's names on one's body.

If Tanaka is correct, tattooing as an expression of devotion and commitment spread from the Ryukyu Island tradition to something done between courtesans and their clients and finally to "star crossed lovers" lovers in general.

Religious Tattoos

During the previous Warring States period 1467-1600, people lived with a general sense that death could come at any moment. This feeling of impending brutality no doubt still permeated the Genna Era of 1615-1624 despite the fact the peaceful Edo Era was under way and Samurai were all too aware that they did not know when and where they may be called upon to give up their life. So they began to tattoo the six letter phrase 南無阿弥陀仏 *Namu Amida Butsu*, a prayer for rebirth in Sukhavati, the Pure Land of Amitabha or the seven letter phrase 南無妙法蓮華経 *Namu Myoho Rennge Kyo* "Glory to the Lotus Sutra" to ensure their soul found happiness after death and that they would have the divine protection of the Buddha.

Looking again in the pages of *The Fun Happy Laughing Reader* we find a tale of a chivalrous man from the Kanto area.

Tsurigane Yasaemon of the Asakusa Sumida River section of Edo was a man of great repute. At the time people with large tattoos were quite rare. He had 南無阿彌陀佛, *the prayer for rebirth in Sukhavati, the Pure   Land of Amitabha: "I believe in the infinite light and the eternal nature of the Amida Buddha," tattooed in big Kanji horizontally across his back, from shoulder to shoulder.*

In the illustration below I have re-created this tattoo using calligraphy by Honen 法然 (1133 –1212), founder of Pure Land Buddhism.

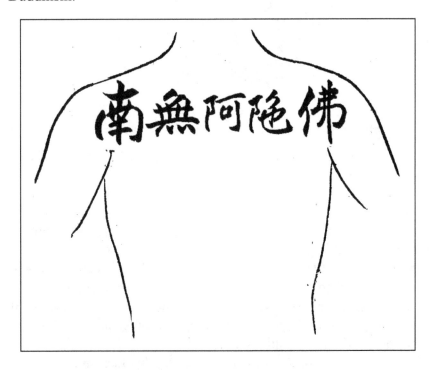

It seems clear that the tattooing traditions in Japan had spread beyond romance to show religious devotion and a desire to protect one's soul in the afterlife. However, this "emergence" of religious tattooing is actually more of a "re-emergence" since tattooing was long practiced by Buddhist monks as part of their Kugyo, painful way devotional practices.

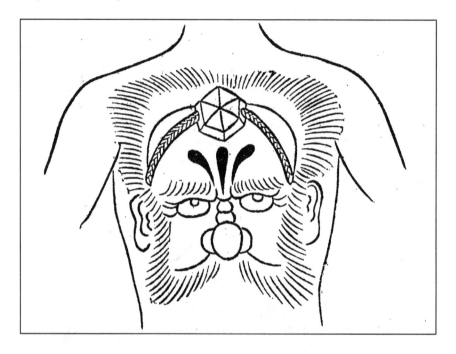

Terada Seiichi in his 1912 study On Tattooing recorded several people with large religious themed tattoos. The illustration (above) shows as Yamabushi, or mountain ascetic, covering the entire back of a person. Though the drawing is simple (or at least Terada's rendering of it is) the image is dramatic. A full face showing an intense face and furrowed brow. On his head the Yamabushi is wearing a small black box tied to his head. This is called a Tokin 頭襟, or "head collar." It serves as both decorative and utilitarian purposes as it can be used as a drinking cup. The Yamabushi practiced Shugendō which is a combination of Shinto, Taoism and other pre-Buddhist worship practices.

He also notes of a man with the seven character mantra of the Nichiren Sect of Buddhism *Namu Myōhō Renge Kyō* or *Devotion to the Mystic Law of the Lotus Sutra.* This was bracketed on either side by the crest of Nichiren Buddhism.

南無妙法蓮華經

The above illustration shows the crests of Nichiren Buddhism on the left and right with *Devotion to the Mystic Law of the Lotus Sutra* in the center. Other Nichiren practitioners tattooed Juzu prayer beads around their neck.

Sumo Wrestlers and Otokodate

In the Genroku Era 1688-1704 tattoos began to expand further as men began to tattoo themselves to show their bravery and fighting spirit. In 1704 book *One Hundred Erotic Poems by One Hundred Poets* the following line appears,

Tattooing is one of the techniques done by Sumo Wrestlers

Sumo wrestler, or Rikishi was not yet a profession in the Genroku Era. Matches were simply between men that wished to challenge each other and compare strength. They arranged bouts themselves and any accompanying people, or people passing by, watched the ensuing Sumo match. Sumo was called Yorizumo 寄相撲, come together Sumo, at this time. The men who participated in these bouts were part of a new group referred to as Otokodate 男伊達, self-styled Robin Hood-like "street knights" or Kyokyaku 侠客 "gentlemen gamblers." They were part of an emerging new class of second or third sons of Samurai (who would not inherit,) banner men with low stipends or sons of well-to-do but low class merchants. They sought to make their living gambling, or at least make it appear that is how they made money. Their motto is often characterized as,

強きを挫き弱きを助ける

Break the strong and help the weak

The merchant class in particular was often more well to do than Samurai families and indeed often lent money to them, despite their significantly lower social status. As the peaceful Edo Era proceeded the Samurai class began to be resented as they were seen as having no responsibility. Samurai paid no taxes and were a protected class, and city dwellers were subject to their whims and abuses. Therefore the Otokodate served as the buffer between the average citizen and the Samurai. They sought to do good deeds, as "street knights" though others were more prone to violence. The latter group were proud of their own strength and liked to show off by taking part in Sumo matches. They began to tattoo themselves and enjoyed the shock that revealing such tattoos brought.

The Otokodate were popular characters in Kabuki dramas that feature them as rather rough Samurai of poor means, who nevertheless are noble in their actions. The illustration above shows the character Nozarashi Gosuke 野晒悟助 by Kuniyoshi. His Kimono was patterned with "skulls that have been left exposed in a field," which what is meant by his name, Nozarashi. He committed himself to helping people in so much trouble it was like pulling grass out of the eyes of weather-beaten skulls.

In *Tales of Old Japan* by Algernon Freeman-Mitford (1803 - 1868) he writes a description of Otokodate (which he, in turn, got from a "Japanese of a native scholar.")

The following two pages reproduce a section from *Tales of Old Japan* titled A Story of the Otokodate of Yedo (Edo). The book is a collection of short stories focusing on Japanese life of the Edo period.

A STORY OF THE OTOKODATÉ OF YEDO ;

BEING THE SUPPLEMENT OF

THE STORY OF GOMPACHI AND KOMURASAKI.

THE word Otokodaté occurs several times in these Tales ; and as I cannot convey its full meaning by a simple translation, I must preserve it in the text, explaining it by the following note, taken from the Japanese of a native scholar.

The Otokodaté were friendly associations of brave men bound together by an obligation to stand by one another in weal or in woe, regardless of their own lives, and without inquiring into one another's antecedents. A bad man, however, having joined the Otokodaté must forsake his evil ways; for their principle was to treat the oppressor as an enemy, and to help the feeble as a father does his child. If they had money, they gave it to those that had none, and their charitable deeds won for them the respect of all men. The head of the society was called its "Father;" if any of the others, who were his apprentices, were homeless, they lived with the Father and served him, paying him at the same time a small fee, in consideration of which, if they fell sick or into misfortune, he took charge of them and assisted them.

The Father of the Otokodaté pursued the calling of farming out coolies to the Daimios and great personages for their journeys to and from Yedo, and in return for this received from them rations in rice. He had more influence with the lower classes even than the officials; and if the coolies had struck work or refused to accompany a Daimio on his journey, a word from the Father would produce as **many** men as might be required. When Prince Tokugawa Iyémochi, the last but one of the Shoguns, left Yedo for Kiyôto, one Shimmon Tatsugorô, chief of the Otokodaté, undertook the management of his journey, and some three or four years ago was raised to the dignity of Hatamoto for many faithful services. After the battle of Fushimi, and the abolition of the Shogunate, he accompanied the last of the Shoguns in his retirement.

In old days there were also Otokodaté among the Hatamotos; this was after the civil wars of the time of Iyéyasu, when, though the country was at peace, the minds of men were still in a state of high excitement, and could not be reconciled to the dulness of a state of rest; it followed that broils and faction fights were continually taking place among the young men of the Samurai class, and that those who distinguished themselves by their personal strength and valour were looked up to as captains. Leagues after the manner of those existing among the German students were formed in different quarters of the city, under various names, and used to fight for the honour of victory. When the country became more thoroughly tranquil, the custom of forming these leagues amongst gentlemen fell into disuse.

The past tense is used in speaking even of the Otokodaté of the lower classes; for although they nominally exist, they have no longer the power and importance which they enjoyed at the time to which these stories belong. They then, like the 'prentices of Old London, played a considerable part in the society of the great cities, and that man was lucky, were he gentle Samurai or simple wardsman, who could claim the Father of the Otokodaté for his friend.

The word, taken by itself, means a manly or plucky fellow.

AN " OTOKODATE " OR " MACHI YAKKO."

男伊達すなわち町奴
Illustration by Inoue Jukichi,井上十吉 1862-1929

A two page scene from *Mt. Gozannokiri* 五三桐山 (date and author unknown) showing a ruffian revealing his heavily tattooed arm in order to get free food and drink. Other customers avert their eyes in fear.

The proprietors preparing food and drink for their fearsome guests.

The Otokodate there were some that tattooed the names of female prostitutes, serving girls, young women and male prostitutes. The tattoos would proceed one by one down first one arm, then the other. If space ran out then Otokodate would tattoo them onto their back, chest and even stomach. Tanaka states,

As we enter the Kyoho Era 1716-1736 we see an increase in tattooing by those people friendly with rough and violent scoundrels, as well as other sorts of ruffians also begin to tattoo themselves in significant number.

Other short passages from Edo Era literature include,

A line within the play *The Woman-Killer and the Hell of Oil* reads,

Men that work as collectors will often have all manner of things tattooed on their bodies. To end arguments they will make as if reaching into their Kimono thereby revealing the markings.

Within the *A Hundred Retired Brothel-Worker's Poems* we can also read the line,

If they try and play the fool, the collector will often roll up his sleeve, proudly exposing a tattooed arm.

It appears from these entries that by the early 18th century tattoos had become more elaborate as they become associated with rough characters. Thugs found they could shock and menace people just by revealing a tattoo. Simply by showing a tattoo they could make their victim more malleable and facilitate their criminal activity. This strategy lead to the increase in more macabre tattoos.

The illustration below shows a collector revealing a Namakubi 生首, or severed head tattoo. The man on the left looks shocked and horrified at the image of a woman's Namakubi. The image is from *A Children's Illustrated Lessons on Life* 児訓影絵喩 by Santo Kyoden 山東京伝.

The Namakubi tattoo can be of either a woman's or a man's head. Typically, if it is a man's head, the forehead will be shaved like a Samurai and the hair on the back of the head will be in disarray, indicating the head was that of a Samurai killed in battle. The meaning of the male severed head is twofold, on one hand it shows your ferocity on the other hand it shows you are willing to die for your beliefs. Taking the head of a warrior in battle would grant the Samurai who took it a certain amount of merit, depending on the level of the warrior. Further, displaying the head of an enemy was a further insult called Sarashi 晒. So getting a Namakubi of a man shows bravery, fearlessness and a warning that you are prepared to do violence.

The latter meaning is usually dedication to your lord or family. The severed head represents the total commitment a person had to his ideal. The story behind the severed head was usually a man who was executed while achieving, or trying to achieve, his goal. The story of Mikenjaku from ancient China who cut his own head off to facilitate his revenge is one example.

On the other hand, female Namakubi typically appear with their hair well ordered. On the other hand the severed head of a woman, typically in the style of a Geisha, has the somewhat contradictory meaning of "even though she works as a courtesan she still is devoted to death to one man."

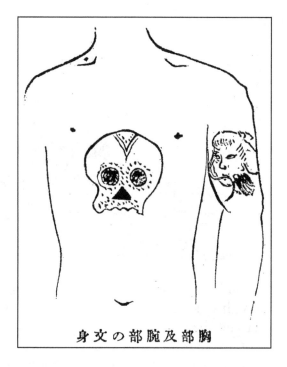

身文の部腕及部胸

Terada Seiichi speculates on the psychology of the severed head tattoo, particularly the woman's severed head. (Illustration above of a Namakubi on the upper left arm of a man and a large Dokoro, or skull on the man's chest.)

It's use as a means of intimidation goes without saying, however it also can express ion passion regarding ones wife or lover. In addition it can also serve as a kind of self-admonition. Though the underlying reasons behind such a tattoo as well as its objective can vary from person to person.

Both male and female Namakubi tattoos are often depicted with a document clenched between the teeth. This scroll is a Zankanjo 斬奸状 or notice of revenge. This letter details why the evil person was killed. A knife driven through the side of the face and top of the head is also a common motif.

I wasn't able to find an Edo Era Zankanjo but there was an incident in 1921 that involved one called the Hara Takashi Assassination 原敬暗殺事件. Hara Takashi was the Prime Minister and he was killed by an employee of the Railroad Department named Nakaoka Ryoichi, who had a history of severely criticizing the Prime Minister. The incident unfolded at 7:25 in the morning on November 4th of 1921, as the Prime Minister was arriving at Tokyo station for a trip to Kyoto. Nakaoka suddenly charged with a Tanto, short sword, and stabbed the Prime Minister Hara in the right side of his chest. The Tanto went through Hara's lung and into his heat, killing him instantly. This is the Zankanjo that Nakaoka wrote:

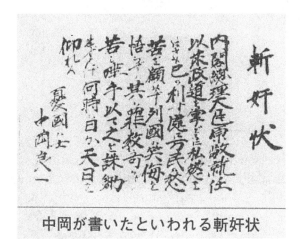

中岡が書いたといわれる斬奸状

Prime Minister Hara Takashi, since you have taken office your policies have been selfish and focused only on enriching yourself. You have no consideration for the suffering of the citizens. You make no effort to rebuke the insults from other countries. There is no excuse for this crime. If some brave hand does not uproot this evil, then we will not be able to look up to the Emperor.

Strangely, after being arrested he was given a life sentence after a rather rapid trial. His sentence was later reduced and in 1934 he was released. He died in 1980 at the age of 77.

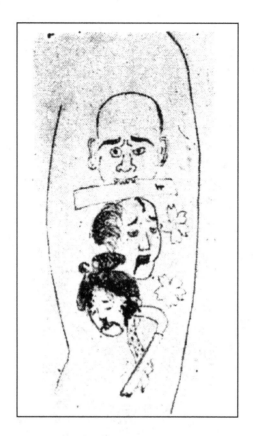

One of the men Terada Seiichi interviewed for his research had this triple Namakubi severed head tattoo (illustration above.) The man who had the tattoo stated that the tattoo, which is on the bicep of his left arm, represents Sakura Sōgorō 佐倉惣五郎.

Sakura Sogoro (1605 –1653), was a Japanese farmer. While many aspects of his life cannot be confirmed, it seems he requested leniency from the Shogun with regards to taxes and handling of bad crop years. Since direct appeals to the Shogun were forbidden Sakura was arrested and his entire family were crucified in 1653 as a warning. Since he was the leader of a peasant rebellion he is admired as a martyr. Sakura is enshrined in Toshoji temple in Narita City.

As can be seen in the above entries, the tradition of tattooing had risen amongst villains, bullies and neer-do-wells from the 1680's until the beginning of the 18th century.

One interesting resource describes a large group of criminals that had been sentenced to "far away banishment" for serious crimes. This punishment usually meant they were sent to the small islands that extend out for hundreds of kilometers from Edo. A man by the name of Mishima Kanuemon三島勘右エ門 travelled to Hachijo Island 300 kilometers from Edo. In his book about the trip *A Detailed Look at the Traditions of the Seven Izu Islands*伊豆七島風土細覧, which was published in 1800, he describes the appearance of 160 people banished due to criminal activity to Hachijo Island.

They have tattooing on their arms and shoulders with no gap between. For example dragons, tigers, plums, bamboo and large letters engraved in. You can also see severed head of women with a scroll in her mouth.

The description of the people who have been convicted of crimes and sent to the island shows a correlation between tattooing culture and criminals at this stage. In addition, Mishima's description seems to indicate extensive tattooing was being done on the upper half of the body. The mix of natural and supernatural imagery along with lettering is interesting to note.

The Namakubi motif certainly does recall the *Memento Mori*, or remembrance of death tokens, carried by medieval Christians.

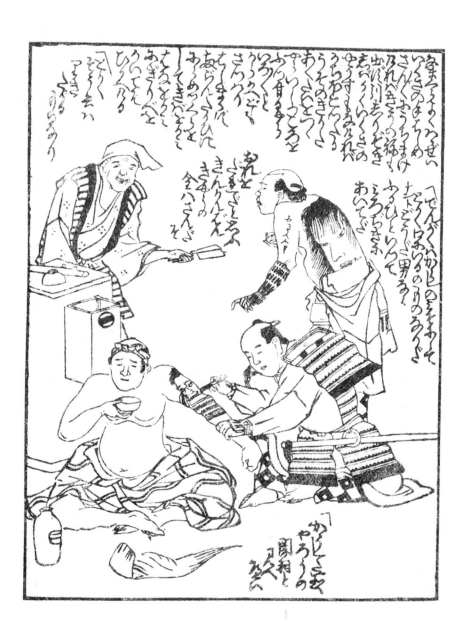

In this panel of the Edo Era manga story *A Grand Brawl Rivalling the Taiheiki* 俠太平記向鉢巻 published in 1797. The story revolves around two groups of Hikeshi Jinsoku, or firefighters' assistants that get into a brawl. The book is based on a true story of the fight that occurred at the 1797 Mountain King festival in Edo between the Ni Group and the Yo Grosup of firefighters. The publication of this book by Shikitei Sanba 式亭三馬 and an unknown artist (possibly from the Utagawa School) actually resulted in additional violence. Due to dissatisfaction with the way they were portrayed in the story the groups involved destroyed the publishing studio and several book stores that stocked the book were ransacked.

This man has an impressive Namakubi of a woman (?) with a Zankansho in her mouth coving his whole back. In addition he has "My life dedicated to [illegible]" on his left arm.

This man is getting a Namakubi tattoo of what appears to be Inokuma with a piece of armor in his mouth. However the tattoo artist is saying,
This is a little bit rough but this guy I'm tattooing on your arm is Guan Yu 關羽 *if anyone asks.*
It is interesting to note that the artist is using several needles tied in a bunch. Both Inokuma and the severed head of a woman appeared in *Mission of the Tattooed Arm.*

Unusual Tattoos

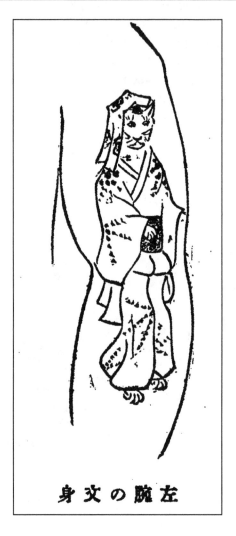

身文の腕左

Tattooing for personal protection or to capture an effect also began to appear. The above illustration of a Bakeneko, a cat in human form, or possibly a Kitsune, fox, (on the left arm) from Terada Seiichi's *On Tattooing*, 1912. If the tattoo is a fox, it probably represents Inari Okamai, the god of fertility, rice, tea and general prosperity. Those that seek worldly success will often have a small shrine to Inari in their house.

In the city of Edo during the Kyoho Era there was a famous hooligan by the name of Kansaburo who had tattooed, in huge letters across his back, *Until death do take me.* 死次第. The illustration below recreates this.

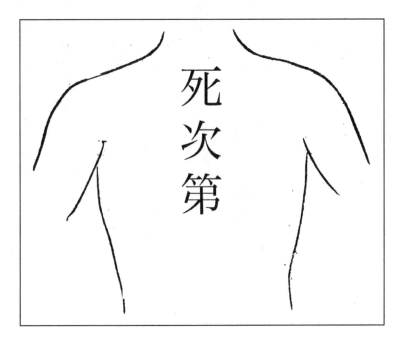

In Horeki Era 1751-1762 *The Fun Happy Laughing Reader* states,

In the years of the Kanreki Era 1748-1751 one could certainly see people with Ukiyo scenes of the floating world as well as the pictures tattooed on the exposed skin of day laborers however for the most part it was the Kanji combination "Isshin" meaning "Completely Dedicated to" or swirls showing little skill or intricacy.

Therefore people from several different classes were getting tattoos of simple phrases and basic designs. Some figures were beginning to be tattooed, and in the case of Namakubi, parts of figures. Some of the more popular phrases were the Buddhist invocation ,

命入八幡大菩薩

Pray to be Granted Life with the Hachiman Buddha referring to the Shinto-Buddhist god of war and protector of the Japanese people, were tattooed into the flesh. Another was Isshin 一心, which means "singlemindedness" or "devotion to a single purpose" and can be tattooed in conjunction with a person's name.

Further, in the comic book, *Idiotic Lectures* we find recorded a person with URINATING IN THIS PLACE FORBIDDEN written in thick, bold Kanji from the top of the shoulder to the tip of the fingers. Whatever the tattooing it seems that for the most part they were simple affairs.

Just as an aside on the rather vulgar tattoo, it turns out it is slightly more cerebral than one would guess at first glance. It is a minor sub story within the 47 Ronin.義士四十七圖. A number of Samurai were out drinking and a high ranking official heard that one person by the name of Sasaki was an expert calligrapher and so he set up a blank, folding screen in order to get him to write a poem about spring flowers. Instead he wrote 此所小便無用 "Do not pee here" As the master was becoming enraged another poet took up a brush and added 花乃山 making the screen read "Here at this mountain the flowers don't need your pee." Together, they make a kind of poem and the master was delighted and made the screen a household treasure. (There are probably some subtleties I'm missing here but amusing all around.)

こんな小型の刺青をよくお風呂などでごらんになるでせう。これは迷信と愛着の部に入るもので右の端は渡邊綱の紋です。次は桃太郎の旗印です。これはともに鬼退治した強い者の印を入れて魔除け、厄年のがれを意味するものである。同じ魔除けでも蛇とか鯉を彫る人もある。蛇は無敵、鯉は強い男とか金太郎を意味するものである。公妓の腕に鯉を彫っている者が多い。これは啓を澤山ハサミ取る頼味である。藝妓や待合の女將

Good Luck Tattoos

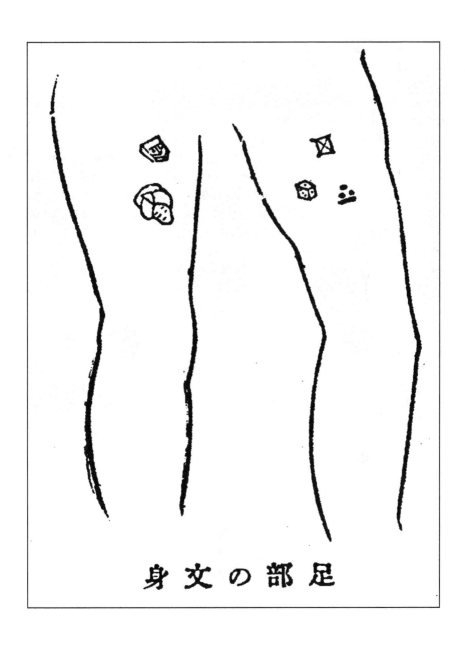

Illustration of a subject with a collection of small tattoos on the legs from *On Tattooing* Terada Seiichi 1912

Simple tattoos done by amateur tattoo artists, the person themselves, or a friend came in many varieties. The subjects tended to be about gambling, girls, and luck. This tradition of tattooing names and simple depictions of good luck symbols extended up through the early 20th century. They were often referred to as Itazura-bori, or goofing off tattoos.

On the previous page Terada Seiichi made this illustration for his book *On Tattooing*, 1912. Terada typically make sketches of the tattoos he saw, but he made no notations on coloring. However we can see the approximate placement and size of the tattoos. On the left is a Shoji, Japanese Chess tile and a woman's head. On the right is a Saikoro, or die (dice.) The box with an X drawn through it may be the Japanese unit of measurement for dry goods known as a Masu. The kanji for the square Masu box is 升 but it is often written as a symbol ☑. The tattoo here is shown as ⊠, so that may be a variation.

Terata Seiichi, who studied the Meishin 迷信 or superstations within the criminal community, found that these simple tattoos were often paired. He discovered that images on one thigh or arm would have their opposite on the other arm. He explains in his 1921 article *An Interest in Writing on the Body* (Tattooing),

*In order to avoid being caught by the police criminals would tattoo a Chochin*提灯, *policeman's lantern on their bodies. This charm would allow them to escape the notice of the police.*

Dr. Terada was a psychologist and published papers about criminal psychology. He noted the types and positioning of tattoos criminals had on their bodies when he interviewed them. One thing he discovered was that candles and bats featured prominently. He theorized the tattoos served the dual function of preventing police from finding the wearer and allowing them to see better at night. Unfortunately, he did not publish any illustrations of bat or candle tattoos.

Koi, or Japanese carp, appear frequently as well. This is because they represent the disposition of the Samurai. They swim upstream and overcome obstacles

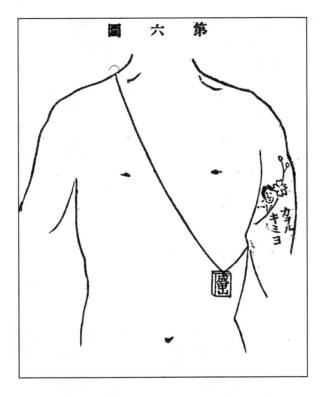

The illustration above shows a common practice Dr. Terada found of combining a charm on a string with a tattoo. The tattooed names "Kaoru and Kimiyo" along with a flower The string holds a talisman from Narita Temple. This connects to the tattoo of the man's girlfriend that he has sliced into his arm, probably with a straight razor.

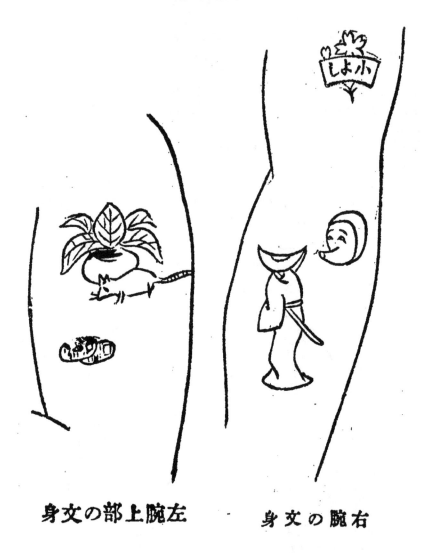

身文の部上腕左　　・　　身文の腕右

Dr. Terada also discussed interesting groupings of small tattoos. The illustration on the left shows a rat beside a turnip and two gold coins. In Japanese the words for turnip and stock (as in stock market) are homophones. So with this tattoo the user seeks to "raise his stock." The illustration is on the upper part of the left arm, from Terada Seiichi's *On Tattooing*, 1912.

The illustration on the right shows the right arm of the same person. This man has three tattoos on his arm, the name Koyoshi, a Samurai and a Hyottoko mask. The Hyottoko mythical spirit masks are often sold at Japanese festivals or worn by dancers. The elongated mouth of the Hyottoko has erotic connotations. Terada Seiichi notes,

Sometimes the tattoos were paired with the images on one arm connecting with the images on the other. Sometimes something feminine would be placed opposite something masculine.

Though he doesn't offer any illustrations Dr. Terada describes two people he interviewed in the early 1900s,

1. Left thigh: a peach
   Right thigh: a Hyottoko mask with an extended mouth
2. Left thigh: a peach and a dolphin
   Right thigh: hot peppers and a penis

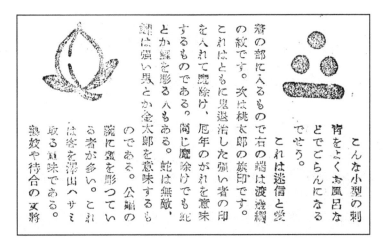

This article from an early 20th century magazine *True Beauty* 艶麗, by Aoyama Saburo 青山三郎, gives some information regarding the small symbols that were popular with Edo Era people.

Many of you are familiar with this little symbols, maybe you have even seen them in the bathhouses. They are used by people who are superstitious or are seeking love. The symbol on the right is the family crest of Watanabe no Tsuna 953 – 1025, who was one of the four great warriors of General Minamoto no Yorimitsu.

The Samurai Watanabe was a pretty tough fellow, while fighting off a demon at Rashomon gate he heroically succeeded in cutting off the monster's arm. One theory is that the crest of the Watanabe household signifies a person who has the power to maim a devil. That is the strength the wearer hopes to gain.

Another theory is that the design represents three eyes. In addition to your own two eyes there is an additional 3rd eye watching out for you. Whether for good or bad you will be that much more sensitive to the conditions around you. Those that believe in the power of such tattoos will feel they are able to respond more nimbly. The article continues,

The simple drawing of the peach is the symbol of Momotaro "Peach Boy" from the fairy tale by the same name. It is known as a mark of strength.

Momotaro who was adopted by an elderly couple after they found him inside a large peach floating down the river, went on to defeat all the demons on Devil Island.

Other people prefer to tattoo snakes or carp onto their bodies. Snakes are invulnerable and cannot be defeated. Carp are the symbol of strong boys, that is why Japanese fly Konobori or carp shaped kites on Children's Day. These types of marks are used by those with a strong desire to remove any curse by an evil spirit. They are used as protection against your Yakudoshi 厄年, or unlucky year.

The unlucky ages for men are when they turn 25, 42 or 61. For women it is 19, 33 and 37 years old. The year before and the year after are also somewhat unlucky and the first signs of unlucky premonitions begin to appear. This is called Maeyaku 前厄. The year after the inauspicious year is called Atoyaku 後厄 wherein the chance of misfortune wanes over the course of that year. Those that are concerned about their inauspicious year can go to a temple or shrine and receive a Yakubarai 厄祓, a talisman to sweep away evil or Yakuyoke厄除け a charm to remove any evil.

The article concludes with the amusing line,

Prostitutes often tattoo crabs on their arms in order to get more clients.

It is unclear if they tattoo the Kanji for crab, 蟹 Kani, or a drawing of a crab. The claws of a crab are called Hasami in Japanese. This is phonetically the same sound as scissors, or to pinch hold of. In this case it means "grab hold of clients."

The illustration above is a Yakeyoke, charm to banish evil, depicting Ryōgen 良源, 912 – 985, who was the head of Enyaku Temple on Mount Hie in Kyoto. He is considered to be the leader who reinvigorated the Tendai sects Buddhism. He is sometimes depicted in a fearful aspect as the Great Horned Teacher 角大師 or the Great Teacher Who Banishes Misfortune 厄除け大師.

Temples sell pieces of paper with the image of Ryōgen on them as charms to banish ill fortune. Even today these charms can be found pasted above the entrances of homes and businesses. There is no direct evidence of this being used as a tattoo but the casual style of the illustration suggests it is certainly possible.

Gambling Related Tattoo Charms

A Meiji Era photograph of a deliveryman. He has a Saikoro, dice, tattooed on his left thigh.

The dice are, as you might expect, relate to gambling. Some of the people that had a Saikoro 賽 tattooed on their bodies were part of a vow to give up gambling but others did it for luck. The game usually played with dice is called Chohan, even or odd. Two dice are shaken in a cup and the cup is then flipped upside down on the table. Everyone bets whether the total of the numbers showing will be Cho or Han, even or odd.

Depending on the situation, the dealer will sometimes act as the house, collecting all losing bets. But more often, the players will bet against each other (this requires an equal number of players betting on odd and even) and the house will collect a set percentage of winning bets. Often the dealer will be wearing only a Fundoshi, or loincloth, to demonstrate he cannot cheat. Since such games were run by the Yakuza his tattoos were on full display.

The dice tattoo invariably had the even numbers hidden with only the odd showing.

In Isogawa Zenchi's *A Study of Tattooing Culture* he found that,

Amongst criminals the most common tattoos were, A woman's name, A human figure, usually from Water Margin and A peach. In fact, out of 215 suspects, 29 had peach tattoos.

Professional gamblers, called Bakuto 博徒, were obviously fans of tattooing symbols in order to bring luck. Bakuto can even be found today. The tradition of tattooing amongst gamblers extends into the present day. There is even a word for tattoo specific to gamblers. It is Kurikara Mon-mon 倶利迦羅紋々 which means "an incarnation of the Lord of Light Fudo as a dragon wrapped around a sword." The illustration below is a recreation of this tattoo with the 1849 woodblock print by Katsushika Hokusai (1760-1849). This deity is unwavering in his commitment to bringing wayward souls into the Buddha's grace.

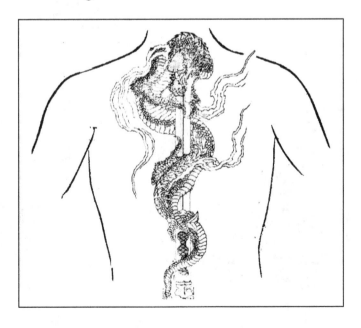

An early manga called *Memory Aid Dictionary for the Illiterate and Dumb* 無筆節用似字尽 first published in 1797 contains an entry involving tattooing. It was written by Kyokutei Bakin 曲亭馬琴(1767-1848) and probably illustrated by Kitano Shigemasa 北尾重政. This illustration is from the 1839 version of the book.

Text at the top:

It is well known that the great Chinese warrior Guan Yu 關羽 (?~220 CE) played a game of Go (I-Go) whilst a poison arrow was being removed from his arm, nowadays gamblers and ruffians drink Sake whist getting a Horimono (tattoo.) The clean, blemish-free skin given to them at birth by their parents is turned into scrap paper with words like *Completely Dedicated To* [something/ someone.] This will cause anything to turn into rubbish.

Horimono-Shi (tattooist)

I'm going to finish this Kurikara with crimson ink, you should drink at least 5 cups of Sake for the pain.

Man

Do a good job and really dig it in! I can't wait to show this off to my friends down at the shore!

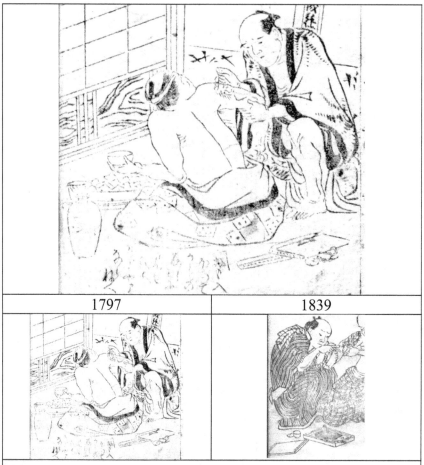

| 1797 | 1839 |

While the text from the 1839 edition of *Memory Aid Dictionary for the Illiterate and Dumb* is the same as the 1797 edition, the illustrations contained new woodblock-prints. When comparing these two versions there are some significant differences in how tattooing is presented. In the 1797 edition the tattoo artist is using a single needle to prick out the design, which is hardly more than an outline. His left hand is just being used to support the arm being tattooed. The kimono of the man is decorated with Saikoro, or dice, indicating he is a gambler. In contrast to this, the 1839 version the hands of the tattoo artist seem to more closely resemble how Wabori, Japanese tattooing is done today. The design is more elaborate and extends over a larger area, with some indication Bokashi filler is being used.

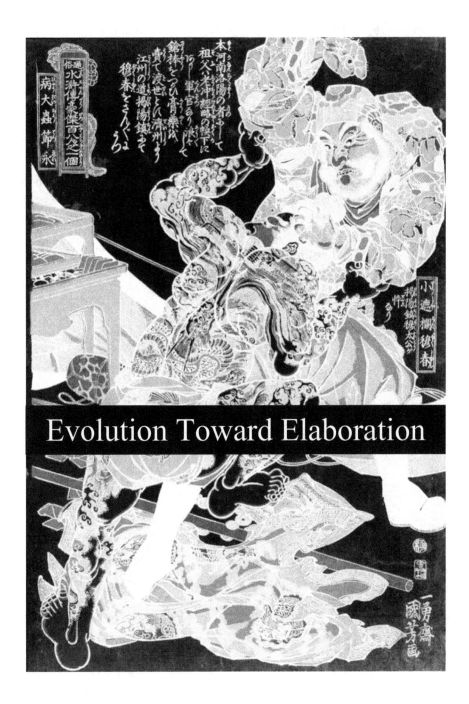

Evolution Toward Elaboration

The five volume *All Manner of Tales from a Wise Monkey* 諸道聴耳世間猿 by Ueda Akinaru 上田秋成 published in 1766, describes a person with landscapes from the famous prints of *Eight Views of Omi* tattooed on his upper arm along with a picture of a Namakubi, severed head, on his back. This blend of natural scenery with *memento mori* is curious to imagine.

Also it states that in Osaka, artwork by the artist and Kabuki playwright Hamamatsu Utakuni's became the subject of tattoos. Horned demon masks from Noh theater, called Hannya became popular. These masks represent jealous female demons and were could be found tattooed on people's arms, chests and stomachs. There were also pictures of the gates of hell and depictions of the long-necked female ghost Rokuro-Kubi

Top: A Rokuro-Kubi 轆轤首 ghost, artist unkown, Edo Era.

Left: A Hannya 般若 mask illustration, artist unknown, Edo Era. This is a mask used to show a woman's vengeful spirt.

Eight Views of Omi by Hiroshige, Edo Era.

Clear breeze at Awazu 粟津晴嵐

Evening glow at Seta 瀬田夕照

Evening rain at Karasaki 唐崎夜雨

Evening snow at Hira 比良暮雪

Geese returning to Katata 堅田落雁

Autumn moon at Ishiyama 石山秋月

Evening bell at Miidera 三井晩鐘

Returning sails at Yabase 矢橋帰帆

It is not entirely clear why the *Eight Views of Omi* are significant. Ueda Akinaru gives his thoughts on tattooing in *All Manner of Tales from a Wise Monkey,*

I heard that long ago in China the peoples of the domains of Go and Etsu covered their entire bodies in tattoos instead of clothing. My understanding is that their entire lives were spend diving into the water and collecting seafood. In Edo the various gangs of Otokodate "Street Knights/ ruffians" are always competing with each other. They will have their entire arms festooned with Iribokuro "tattooed moles" or even have their whole torsos covered with dragons. Sometimes on their back you will see the severed head of Mikenjaku.

Note: Mikenjaku 眉間尺 was the son of a famous swordsmith husband and wife team in China around 771 to 476 BCE. The Emperor ordered them to make a pair of swords for him in 3 months, but they failed, so and the emperor had them killed. The son, Mikenjaku, swore revenge but was unable to complete the task. He then cut his own head off for an assassin to present to the emperor as evidence of success. As the emperor stared into the eyes of the dead Mikenjaku the assassin cut his head off.

On the side of their buttocks they would have Eight Views of Omi. The Fever pitch tattooing had reached was such that if the great Buddhist monk Kukai (Kobo Daishi) had so desired someone could have tattooed all 600 scrolls of Secret Key to the Heart Sutra on his body.
As to the motivations, I would say that the men coming up from Osaka or Kyoto, the old capital, give off a sense of being only lukewarm in power. They are completely satisfied with the body they were born into and don't want to change. They think they can just pass as a man in this city, but Edo isn't like that.

This is perhaps saying that while tattooing started in the pleasure quarters of the Osaka and Kyoto area, in Edo it had evolved steadily over the intervening years.

The construction of Azuchi Castle 安土城 may have played a role in the fame of the *Eight Views*. The warlord Oda Nobunaga wanted a castle that would impress and intimidate so he had Azuchi Castle built just outside Kyoto in Omi. It was both lavish and foreboding with an octagonal keep. Looking at the placement of the castle, near lake Biwa, and the fact that its uppermost floor was 8 sided seems to suggest the *Eight Views* are associated with this castle that symbolized Oda Nobunaga's conquest of the other domains. Though some of the views are quite distant and not arranged radially from the castle, the connection with the man that brought all of Japan under his control seems a likely reason such tattooing would be done. The castle was burned down after the betrayal of Nobunaga by one of his lieutenants, Akechi Mitsuhide, in 1582 just three years after completion.

Through these examples it is clear people were having both larger and more complex tattoos done. Further, as the Kansei Era 1789-1801 began, Kinpira Joruri puppet theater plays became the source of design ideas for tattoos. Kinpira Joruri puppet plays were started by the Kabuki actor Ichikawa Danjuro 1675 –1704. Soon, scenes related to his pioneering Aragoto performances, a section of

Kabuki plays that use exaggerated gestures, costumes, makeup, language and movement, began to be used as raw material for tattoos. Thus the traditional arts of the Ichikawa family began to be used as inspiration.

People began to get first the faces and then the entire body of a Kabuki or Joruri play tattooed on their body. In the 1803 book *Essays Through the Years* talks, somewhat disparagingly, about the prevalence of tattooing,

Steeplejacks, known as Tobi in Japanese, as well as the other such people who typically work more or less naked often have dreary illustrations carved into the flesh of their arms which appears to be black as ink. No doubt they see them as tasteful tributes to their mothers and fathers in blues and reds however, they are quite miserable looking.

The references above lead to the conclusion that in the in a relatively short time, beginning in the Meiwa Era in 1764 and extending to the end of the Kyowa Era in 1804 the art of tattooing developed rapidly. In forty years, tattoo progressed from simple monochrome phrases, designs and figures to large multicolored works. Also that men working outside, such as carpenters, roofers and porters, traditionally clothed only in a loincloth, began to tattoo the exposed flesh as a mark of their trade.

The following section will show examples of these tradesmen and their tattoos.

Construction workers, Firefighters, Steeplejacks and Porters

Following the advancements up through 1804, the remainder of the Edo Era, up through the Meiji Restoration in 1868 tattooing became part of the everyday scenery. Workers could be found festooned with tattoos, particularly those who toiled semi-naked in loincloths called Fundoshi. Carpenters and porters and those involved in difficult or dangerous work like firefighters and steeplejacks, called Tobi.

Porters/ Day laborers

A hand-tinted print by Erwin Bälz. Bälz (1849 –1913) was a German anthropologist and the personal physician to the Japanese Imperial Family. He is a cofounder of modern western medicine in Japan.

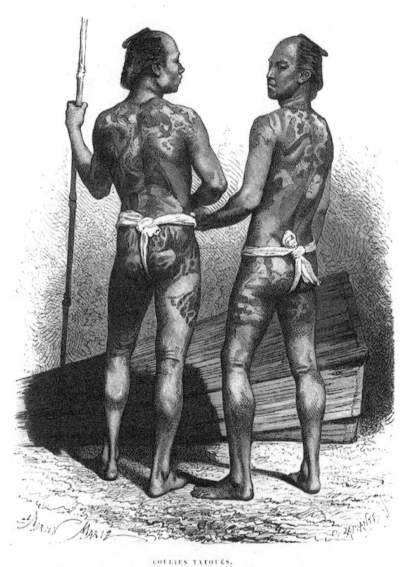

COULIES TATOUÉS.

Tattooed Porters, 1870
Illustration by Aime Humbert 1819-1910

Tobi Steeplejacks

In the illustration on the previous page by Utagawa Kunisada 1864 shows Tobi, or steeplejacks, at work. Tobi refers to the Japanese bird the black kite鳶 which move nimbly from branch to branch of trees. These men worked on high scaffolding hammering together roof joists. You can see some evidence of tattooing on their arms. Like other workers they tattooed themselves partly as decoration, partly to show their bravery and party as a way to intimidate others. There is a famous quote associated with the Tobi,

女房を売っても彫物をする
I will sell my wife and used the money for Horimono

In fact, tattooing became quite necessary. If a person working as a Tobi did not have any tattoos, he would be ridiculed and called a Tukiya搗き屋 a rice polisher, the kind of work only a dull person would do.

Tobi were also active in firefighting. The city of Edo was a large, densely packed city of wood and paper structures. Fires started fast and spread fast. In addition, firefighting at the time was simple. Houses on fire were abandoned and "firefighting" mainly consisted of destroying structures around the fire in order to prevent the flames from spreading. Since Tobi worked on the top of houses they would work at tearing down rooves.

Unfortunately, various groups of Tobi and firefighters, got into fights over who would be in charge of the scene. Other times whole fire departments would start huge fights like the *Mekumi Fight of 1805*, and the *Wogumi and Chigumi Fight of 1818* both of which involved large groups of Tobi (working as firefighters) battling Sumo wrestlers. Both of these incidents were later made into Kabuki plays. This led many in Edo to believe that the Tobi actually rather enjoyed fighting. There is even a famous saying that goes,

火事と喧嘩は江戸の華
Fires and fights are the flowers of Edo

Firefighters

Since fires were a big problem in Edo the government assigned Samurai families to be in charge. The policy, which was created in 1658 in response to a big conflagration the previous year, designated four families as Jobikeshi 定火消, designated firefighters. These were also known as Buke Bikeshi 武家火消, or Samurai Family Firefighters, and were the "official" firefighters of Edo. Local areas also created their own voluntary firefighting organization, which were largely comprised of steeplejacks, construction workers along with other citizens. Those groups were known as Machibike 町火消 village firefighters.

Steeplejacks and construction workers were already well known for being extensively tattooed so the correlation between tattoos and firefighting is just coincidental in their case. In addition, their activity as Machikeike was not their primary profession. The Samurai Family Firefighters were also probably not tattooed, due to their status, however they employed commoners (non-Samurai class) known as Hikeshi Ninsoku 火消人足, or firefighting staff. These firefighters probably did most of the dangerous work as their title was Gaen 臥煙, or those who fall before the smoke. The Gaen were famous for wearing only a loincloth and short Hanten 袢纏 coat, in both summer and being covered with tattoos, which they referred to as Horimono, engravings. These men were employed as full-time firefighters but they supplemented their salaries by going to business and selling "good-luck charms" to prevent fires. These charms were known as Zenisashi 銭緡, or coins on a string. A bunch of low denomination coins were threaded with a hemp cord and then tied off. The Gaen firefighters were famously aggressive when selling these charms and even implied that business that did not purchase one might find their shop getting torn down "by accident" if there was a fire even in the vicinity. They were not well liked by local businesses. Groups of Gaen firefighters often got into scuffles with the steeplejacks and carpenters that made up the village firefighter divisions.

While the Gaen firefighters also enjoyed fighting amongst themselves, the biggest brawls broke out at the scene of a fire. The first group to arrive at the scene would hang their Keshifuda, a wooden name board painted with the company's logo character, from the roof of a nearby house. A firefighter would then climb onto the roof of a nearby house with Matoi 纏, a decorated signal pole. This signal pole would signal other firefighters the location of the blaze and simultaneously stake claim on the honor of being the ones to extinguish the fire. The start of fights tended to occur when a group that arrived later, took down the Keshifuda or Matoi and replaced it with their own, thereby usurping any honor. The illustration below by Utagaw Yoshitora shows a firefighter of the "Se" group standing with his unit's Matoi. He is heavily tattooed and has his firefighting coat tied around his waist showing off his extensive tattooing.

A tattooed firefighter preforming acrobatics atop a bamboo firefighting ladder. Edo Era, artist unknown. 錦絵貼り合わせ

Carpenters

I was not able to find any information regarding tattooing amongst carpenters. Illustration *Mysterious Revolving Tales for Children* 童謡妙々車 Ryukatei Tanekazu and Utagawa Kunisawa. It shows a carpenter with elaborate floral tattooing extending all the way down the arm to the wrists.

Fishermen

I was not able to find any information regarding tattooing amongst fisherman. This illustration shows a fisherman with two Kanji tattoos. The first one is 百 meaning one hundred. The second one is illegible. Illustration from *Tobiya a Family Business* 親父布子鳶握 3 巻 By Ichiba Tsusho 市場通笑, 1739-1812
Illustrations by Torii Kyonaga 鳥居, 清長, 1752-1815

Palanquin Carriers

A PALANQUIN AND ITS BEARERS.

Both palanquin bearers and rickshaw pullers were famous for being heavily tattooed. Such men soon found that being fully tattooed enabled them to acquire more customers. Tanaka found,

Those customers looking to visit Edo's Yoshihara Red Light District tended to select palanquins carried by porters with tattoos. They even tended to select palanquins whose carriers that had the most exquisite and dynamic tattoos.

Rickshaw Drivers

Photo circa 1900.

It became common for rickshaw drivers to get tattooed. Tattooed rickshaw drivers were popular with people travelling to the red light district.

Erwin Bälz

Interesting there is a German doctor that was in Japan in the early part of the Meiji Era and he had an anthropological interest in tattooing. Erwin Bälz (13 January 1849 – 31 August 1913) was a German anthropologist and physician. He became the personal physician to the Japanese Imperial family is is credited with cofounding modern western medicine in Japan. He recorded some observations and interviews he had with Japanese people regarding tattooing.

He recorded in his 1883 book,

Japanese call tattooing Horimono. Over the course of the last 1000 years all countries that have achieved a high level of civilization have abandoned tattooing. On the other hand, tattooing is practiced widely in Japan and has even been elevated to an art form.

Starting about 10 years ago tattooing dramatically increased in popularity amongst the general populous. Just in the city of Tokyo it is said that there are over 30,000 people with tattoos. German sailors will frequently tattoo the ends of their fingers or the backs of their hands, however Japanese will tattoo the torso and all four limbs with large tattoos. One thing it is important to note is that the Japanese do not tattoo the head, neck, hands or feet.

Tattooing is limited to the lower classes and is centered on construction workers, porters and rickshaw drivers. The higher cases view tattooing as shameful. In fact, to put it bluntly, it is hard to find a craftsman or laborer without tattooing. Tattooing has become such a part of the culture that it would be unusual to spot such a person.

In other cultures you find facial and hand tattooing but this is because the rest of the body is covered with clothes. However if a Japanese person with a tattoo puts on a Kimono it would, in fact, entirely cover the artwork and only skin would be visible. Long ago workers would tattoo flies or dragonflies on their shaved tops of their heads as an attempt at humor. However, after talking to Horimono-shi, or tattoo artists, I learned that they don't consider that to be part of real tattooing.

Over the course of my investigation of tattooing I interviewed 25 men. Out of that 25 not a single one had a facial, head or hand tattoo.

Conversely, the Ainu people follow the exact opposite pattern to the Japanese. They tattoo only the hands, forearms and lips. I think this is a significant point. Also in the Ainu culture only women do tattooing. This is similar to the Inuit and eastern Yakut cultures which also live in colder, northern regions.

Erwin Bälz also asked Japanese people about tattooing and recorded their responses.

There is no doubt that tattooing came from china. China used tattooing as a form of punishment. However, this story is very suspect. In Japan, under the Tokugawa Shogunate 1603-1867, the tradition of using a Rakuin 烙印, or brand on prisoners existed for a long time. However, the Rakuin brand consisted only of a circle done around the elbow. Why did the Rakuin give way to tattooing?

In Japan, only people doing certain kinds of work have tattoos. If you look at other professions, there is no tattooing being done. It is not clear why this is so. Even scholars who talk about how Rakuin brands were used on criminals cannot explain how this transition unfolded historically.

I invited a person who had been tattooed 30 years ago to tell me what he thogut about this problem.

"Why did you decide to get a tattoo?" I asked him.
He cocked his head to the side, and replied, "I don't know."
I then asked,
"In the city and alongside the main roads I often see people of a certain class with tattoos, what is the reason for this."
He replied,
"If you don't have enough money for a kimono at least you have your Niku-juban, or "meat jacket and pants." If you don't have at least that a man would be ashamed."

-Erwin Bälz *Die Korperlichen Eigenschaften der Japaner* Yokohama, 1883.
Note: My translation is actually a translation of the Japanese 日本人の身体的特性 by Yasuda Tokutaro 安田徳太郎 in his 1952 book 人間の歴史 2.

Kabuki Actors

Ichikawa Danzo as The Bandit Jiraiya. Utakawa Kuniyoshi 1834.

Kabuki theater was very popular in the Edo era. Surprisingly, a Kabuki actor is credited with adding to the popularity of tattooing. The fourth generation Nakamura Utauemon was a man of small stature and felt his presence had no impact. When preparing for his role as Denshichi Kyurohe he decided to tattoo his entire torso instead of using paint. It was apparently a rip roaring success. In addition, for the September 1834 Nakamura performance he added another tattoo. As he was performing the Kyogen, or wild speech, he revealed a large tattoo of a Kurikura, or a dragon wrapped around a flaming sword. This tattoo on his arm again brought the house down. The impact of the tattoo was something to celebrate rather than to inspire fear.

Courtesans

Tattooing by courtesans in the red light district known as Yoshihara had developed as well. Early tattoos consisted primarily of names and the occasional curse, however the both the subject matter and complexity began to increase as the Edo Era flowed along. Prostitutes got tattooed out of vanity, to intimidate and for good luck. The mix of tattoos was apparently rather extreme with sexual scenes mixed in and around the family crests of favored men. There were also debauched scenes people tattooed on themselves.

In the Shitamachi area of Edo there was a female prostitute by the name of O-Tama who a great number of tattoos. Even if she was with a client once, she would tattoo his family crest on her body. In the book *Considering Tattooing* it states that,

Her back and stomach were completely covered with the family crests of merchants, Samurai and even temple priests and teachers.

Further, there was also O-Kaku, a ruthless woman who specialized in extortion. Her entire body was covered head to toe in a variety of tattoos. In particular it is said she had a flat-headed clawed water demon known as a Kappa tattooed on her body. One of its fingers was extended towards her nether regions. Once, when she was trying on clothing in a high class ladies' wear shop known as Omaruya, she was seen naked by people passing the shop as she

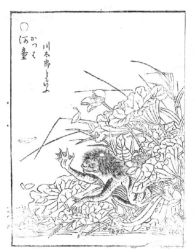

was being fitted. They burst out laughing upon seeing her tattooed body. The story goes, according to *Morisada's Book of Entertaining Tales*, that she then demanded compensation from them for putting on a show.

Illustration of Kappa from the *The Illustrated Night Parade of a Hundred Demons*by Toriyama Sekien1776.

163

Tattooing by women was not just limited to courtesans. In the Hongo Haruki Town of Edo there was a delivery girl by the name of O-Take, little bamboo, who had committed to such an unparalleled level of tattooing that all of Edo City shook and even the violent ruffians of the time found her fearsome. What she had was a tattoo of Kintaro, the boy of supernatural strength and befriender of animals, extending across her back, across her stomach and up to her breast. The mouth of Kintaro, who was all carved in crimson, was open and positioned so that it appeared to be taking her nipple into his mouth. The area around the nipple is particularly sensitive and transmits a more intense pain and this, coupled with the fact that the entire work was done with crimson, which naturally increases the pain, meant that her endurance to pain and suffering was viewed with awe. Even the brutes and rough characters of the area viewed her with fear and accorded her a good measure of respect.

Tattooing in the Samurai Class

By the 1800's tattooing was a common sight amongst steeplejacks, carpenters, actors Sumo wrestlers and courtesans. The Samurai class with the exception of some Otokodae seemed to not take any part. However the book *Tattoo Stories* by Yamanaka Kyoko gives several examples of high ranked Samurai with tattoos.

In August of the eight year of Tenpo,1837, a Daimyo, or regional administrator, by the name of Uchida Ise no Mamori Masakata was forced into retirement due to a charge of misconduct levied against him. This Daimyo, who was in charge of the Shimosa Omigawa Domain, worth ten thousand Koku of rice per year, was said to have been tattooed with all manner of pictures and designs.

Kyoko does not clarify if there is any connection between the tattooing and being replaced as regional administrator, but it seems likely.

Another case mentioned by Kyoko is about a police officer named Toyama Saemon Kagemoto. Police officers in the Edo Era were Samurai. This particular officer, referred to affectionately as

Toyama Kin San, apparently got on the wrong track as a youth. Kyoko says,

In his depraved and debauched youth when his name was Kinshiro he got a tattoo of a woman's Namakubi, or severed head, on his arm.

Finally, Kyoko mentions a man known as the Lord of the South Sea. His real name was Matsudaira Munenobu, who was rather famous for having tattoos.

In addition he had his wife's handmaids get flowers tattooed across their bodies. In the summer they would wear simple silk gauze along with a light Kimono so that the artwork could be seen through the clothing. Following the death of the Guardian of Dewa it turns out that he had a clause in his will that would grant a thousand gold coins to anyone who would take the handmaids into their service. It is said that no one took the offer.

Ukiyo Artists

Ukiyo-e 浮世絵 Floating World Art refers to woodblock prints made in the Edo Era. These cheap prints which became popular in the mid 1600's captured famous Kabuki actors, Sumo wrestlers as well as historic scenes and erotica. Scenes of everyday life and festivals were also common. The triptych below is titled *Pilgrims Readying to Climb Mt. Fuji* 富士登山諸講中之図 by Utagawa Kuniyoshi 1798-1861. It depicts various groups readying to climb Mt. Fuji. In the lower left are the more traditional pilgrims with white clothing, hats and walking sticks. They are looking nervously at the more rowdy types who have extensive tattooing. The men with tattoos could be a group of firemen out on a summer pilgrimage to Mt. Fuji. The moon is out and many are holding lanterns so presumably this is an evening departure to end up at the peak for the rising sun.

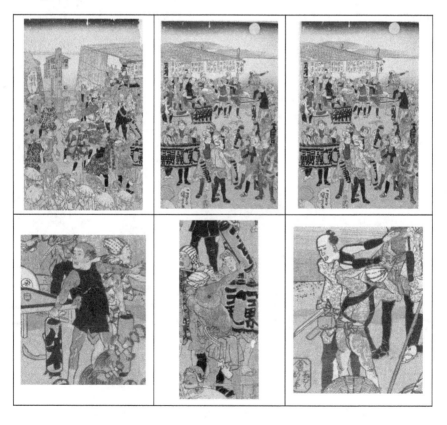

Suiyokuden: Water Margin and Its Influence

Many researchers have indicated that the Ukiyo-e woodblock illustrations by Utakawa Kuniyoshi really pushed tattooing to new heights. Specifically his illustrations for each of the characters in the Chinese adventure tale *Water Margin*. A new translation of *The Water Margin* captured the public imagination and various editions were published continuously up through the Meiji Restoration in 1868. The 108 heroes in this book were posed dramatically and most all featured extensive tattooing. In particular characters like Shi Jin "Nine Dragon Tattooed" (*on the back cover) became famous and people began to correlate tattoos with heroes and heroic action. This matched well with the Otokodate aesthetic and may have given rise to getting one large tattoo as opposed to multiple smaller tattoos.

The themes of Utagawa's prints were raging tigers, dragons, great serpents, thunder gods and Chinese guardian lion-dogs. His brave, bold and fierce illustrations grew in popularity and sold so well that the youth growing up in Edo took those rousing images of valiant warriors and, combined with the astonishing exquisiteness of the tattooing being done at the time, the result was the fashion of using his art as the basis for tattoos. The dragons, cherry blossoms and peonies featured in the illustrations became popular tattoo motifs in addition to the main characters.

The following pages reproduce the illustration of Lu Zhishen 魯智深 from an 1829 edition of *Water Margin* 稗史水滸伝 by Santo Kyosan 山東京山 and illustrated by Utagawa Kuniyoshi. The flowered tattooing across his back features prominently and seems to be set counterpoint to the object of Lu's fury. The practice of tattooing a character with tattoos probably started around this time. In Japanese this is called Niju-bori 二重彫.

The collected works of Kagawa Utayoshi became something of a standard reference book for tattoo artists. As the people of the time saw and appreciated his work it served to increase the popularity of tattooing. Gentlemen and gamblers alike got their entire body covered in imposing tattoos. The intervening skin was also filled in with peonies, waves or cherry blossoms so that hardly any skin showed.

Van Gulik proposes that it the images of the Tattooed heroes from the Water Margin series were so influential that they were directly responsible for the rise of the professional tattoo artist.

The response of the public to the popular tattooed heroes of the Suikoden novel so vividly depicted in the woodblock print series and in the book illustrations dealing with this theme, paved the way for the subsequent rise of professional tattoo masters.

It is curious to note that the author Matsuda Osamu records in his book *A Critical Look At Japanese Tattooing* 日本刺青論1989,

I looked at the illustrations in the Chinese editions of the Suikoden and was surprised at how little tattooing the characters had. Most had none and even the famous Shi Jin "Nine Dragon Tattooed" and a few others had only minor tattoos showing. One edition from the Ming dynasty (1368–1644), that was 100 volumes, had no illustrations and another from the same era, that had 120 volumes, had illustrations but none with tattoos. A 70 volume set from the Qing dynasty (1644 to 1912) had many illustrations but only a few famous characters had tattooing evident, and then very minor.

Illustrations from an Chinese edition of *Water Margin* 忠義水滸全書 by Sū Naian 施耐庵 with art by Rō Koanchion 羅貫忠 (1341-1368.)

Newly Revised and Illustrated Water Margin 新編水滸画伝. By Kyokutei Bakin 曲亭主人 illustrated by Katsushika Hokusai 葛飾北斎.

The popularity and quality of Ukiyo-e art declined after 1868, and later editions of *Water Margin* began to feature less elaborate illustrations. Below is a comparison tattooed characters from *Colloquial Water Margin* 通俗水滸伝 By Utagawa Kuniyoshi (early 1800's) and an edition by Onishi Shonosuke 1885.

The *Water Margin* books no doubt added fuel to the fire but there is clear evidence that the culture of tattooing was well advanced in Edo. 伊豆七島風土細覧 by Mishima Kanuemon 三島勘右エ門 Describes 160 people banished "long distance" due to criminal activity to Hachijo Island. The island is several hundred kilometers directly south of Edo. The description of the people who have been convicted of crimes and sent to the island shows a correlation between tattooing culture and criminals at this stage.

They have tattooing on their arms and shoulders with no gap between. For example dragons, tigers, plums, bamboo and large letters engraved in. You can also see severed head of women with a scroll in her mouth.

In addition, a definition of tattooing from 1782 adds some interesting information. *The Dictionary of Chinese Vernacular* 雅俗漢語訳解 contains the following definition for 刺字 Shiji, "letters pierced into the skin,
    Criminals arrested for the first or second time for robbing or stealing will be tattooed with the two lines on the upper arm. For people caught embezzling funds this punishment will be relaxed. ..What these people have is called Irezumi. On the other hand, people that used a needle to stab the shape of a dragon in blue all over their body like Nine Dragons from Water Margin call that Horimono.

This definition is the first to differentiate between Irezumi, a punishment tattoo, and Horimono, a tattoo done for other reasons. The 108 characters who were all brigands, and tattooed as such matched perfectly with the Otokodate aesthetic. On the fringes but acting heroically.

Meeting of the Tattooing Association

The Tenpo Era 1830-1844 seems to be the time when tattooing achieved its greatest popularity. It was around this time that professional tattooists began to emerge to meet the demand for increasing complex designs. At this point the clientele was rather large, encompassing laborers, courtesans, professional gamblers as well as the occasional curious Samurai. For some of these groups tattooing was so pervasive that not having "an engraving" was basically shameful. There was even a jester's song that went,

Though they may laugh at us when we are old, those that seek to be steeplejacks like us have to have ink.

The names of some of the master tattoo artists in Edo are :

- Charifumi of Asakusa
- Taninaka no Ki
- Namiki of the Carved Rock
- Kamiyui Daruma-Kin
- Yatsuhira of Pine Island Town
- Karakusa Kenta of Asakusa
- Kon-Kon Jiro
- Taninaka Nakakado no Ken
- Yatsupei

I was not able to confirm the readings of these names, but some of their specialties are recorded.

Taninaka no Ki was known for his depictions of Yamauba, a kind of mountain witch, as well as the mighty Kintaro. Illustration of a Yamauba (below) by Sawaki Suushi 佐脇嵩之, from the 1737 *Illustrated Book of One Hundred Ghouls*.

Namiki of the Carved Rock had found a method for rendering figures that made him famous. Kamiyui Daruma-Kin, who was left-handed, nevertheless became famed for his style. Moreover his use of the Bokashi, or fill work (such as cherry blossoms, peonies etc..) was legendary. His dragon tattoos were also famed far and wide.

Karakusa Kenta developed his own Karakusa pattern that he used in his tattoos. He was particularly adept at adding crimson.

An example of a Karakusa pattern used in Japan. The tattoo artist Karakusa Kenta probably used a kind of interlocking pattern based on this.

Yatsupei gathered together the youths living in the Chiyoda section of Edo and tattooed them in honor of the Sanno Matsuri, or Festival of the Mountain King. He even engraved tattoos into his own child, a boy of fourteen. In a fantastic display of brutality, when the boy began to cry due to being unable to endure the pain, Yatsupei had him lashed to a ladder and continued tattooing until the work on the boy was completed.

Tanaka records another striking episode relating to festivals,

It is probably safe to say that nowhere else in the world could match the scene at the Asakusa Three Temple festival whereupon twenty youths leapt forward and formed a line. Baring their backs they revealed a single dragon tattooed across all their backs.

An image of what that might look like

In addition, to these professional engravers there was typically another person who designed the tattoo. Typically they were Ukiyo "Floating World" artists who drew the designs. These people were referred to as Zuanka or designers who would make the initial drawing. Artists like Kagawa Kuniyoshi as well as his disciples, Yoshitsuya, Yoshitora and so on created a great number of these preliminary drawings. It is even said the great painter Katsushika Hokusai drew pictures for tattoos from time to time. Sometimes the tattooing would be divided into a person who did the Gaku or outline and another tattooist who would do the Bokashi or fill and shading.

Typically the way in which tattooing was done did not involve drawing the design on the body itself but referring to an outline on paper whilst working, thus the master engraver did not need to be proficient in drawing original art. Thus Horimono-shi, or Master engravers like *Namiki of the Carved Rock* had a person working with him who was skilled at drawing figures. All of these artisans used ideas from Ukiyo artists, whether it was for the actual art to be tattooed or for reference. Probably the most widely used book was the *One-Hundred Heroes* by Utagawa Kuniyoshi, which was a compilation of the character sheets for all the Water Margin characters.

Irezumi-shi, or tattoo masters, began to form their own organizations and hold meetings to exchange ideas and show off their work. In the Tenpo Era 1830-1844 the Tattooing Association held an event in the Ryogoku section of Tokyo. Tanaka records that,

All the association members arriving sported the most spectacular designs and they debated the relative superiority or inferiority of each. Amongst the participants was a man with a Tanto short knife tattooed onto his stomach. When wearing a Fundoshi loin cloth it appeared as if he were carrying a sheathed knife. Another person had a small Ushiwaka Maru, the name the 12th Century Samurai Minamoto no Yoshitsune had as a youth, tattooed on his left shoulder. Then, under that from his upper arm to elbow he had a tattoo of Benkei, the legendary warrior monk with whom he had a duel.

There was also the man with a spider web tattooed on his head just at where the hairline. A spider, tattooed on the shoulder, hangs from a single strand of that web. However the tattoo that brought

the house down and clearly took the podium was the one sported by a monk. On the head of his penis was tattooed a single wasp.

Seeing as how those daring to going forth and having a large, dramatic tattoo done must have a strong spirit, determination and ability to endure, a lot of times it was crime-lords, head of Sumo Schools or head steeplejacks that had them. By doing so they earned the junior members' respect and admiration. Gentlemen and gamblers who sought to the highest level of status would also get large dramatic images beautifully done on their bodies.

They used their ink for vanity, to threaten or intimidate or show off that they were a pimp. The images tattooed were those of Samurai, the dueling dragon and tiger, severed heads as well as ghosts and ghouls, anything that showed strength. The themes of fierceness and the macabre tended to dominate while the more sedately beautiful flowers, birds mountains and streams were scarce. Some of the tattoos were due to superstition as well. For example a person wanted to have the same all-conquering power as the fairy tale Momotaro "Peach Boy" who subjugated the demons on Onigashima "Island of Devils" and thus got a peach tattooed on their body. Also we have the person who wished to emulate the heart of the dragon rising to heaven so they got a dragon carved into their back and arm. There were also those that tattooed onto their bodies Jiraiya, the shapeshifting Ninja as well as the Samurai Kintaro "Golden Boy" and other such larger than life heroes. Finally there was a certain thief who, in order to see better during his nighttime activities, desired to have a dragonfly etched into his flesh.

Getting a Tattoo

This section is a translation of Tanaka Kougai's explanation of the tattooing process in the Edo Era.

There were apparently two ways to have a tattoo done in this era. The first was visiting the tattooists shop at regular intervals while the second involved staying at the home of the Horimono-shi until the work was completed. The process of performing tattooing surgery involved first making the washing the body thoroughly then drawing the outline. Several fine needles known as Komachi小町 "Small Town" would be bound together to do the outline work. Color fill, or Bokashi, would be done with a Bokashi tool, which is a larger bunch of needles bound together. This type of work can cause rather intense pain. A typical day will consist of some six or seven hundred needle thrusts. Exceeding this amount will cause even the hardiest of people intense discomfort and fatigue.

During the period of time that tattooing is being done you should refrain from overeating or overdrinking. Further, engaging in sexual relations with the opposite sex is forbidden. If a person were to engage in sexual intercourse it is said that the crimson ink used would change in color. Following the tattooing "surgery" you should immediately get in the bath. As this will cause considerable pain, when you finally do crawl out of the bath you will probably lay flat out for twenty minutes or more until the pain subsides enough for you to move. When you eventually feel that you can rise a person will help you up and gently dress you in a Kimono.

Tattooing Implements

This section is primarily a translation of a section of Tamabayashi Haruo's (1898 – 1945) book *The Hundred Shapes of Tattooing* that he published in 1941.

The handle of the tattooing tool is made of sandalwood, ivory or bone. For the most part these materials are used for slimmer handles. If a thicker handle is necessary then bamboo is the most frequently used material.

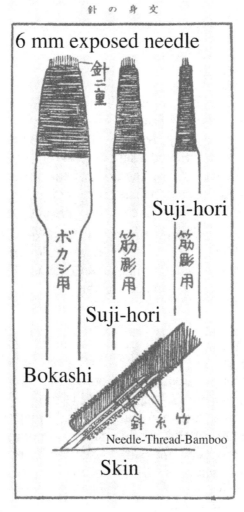

針　の　身　文

6 mm exposed needle

Suji-hori

Suji-hori

Bokashi

Needle-Thread-Bamboo

Skin

In the Edo Era there were needles made specifically for tattooing but these disappeared after the Meiji Restoration in 1868. Following that, most artists used the same needles as the ones for sewing silk, though there were a few famous Horimono-shi that had needles specially made that were thinner.

For most outline work a bundle of 5-11 needles are wrapped around the end of the handle and tied with silk thread, but for particularly fine work as few as 3 could be used. When using 11 or more needles it is common to arrange them in two rows, with 6 on top and 5 below. For particularly large sections of fill-work up to 45 needles can be used. The first row of needles is even and then next odd, so that the needles furthest away and those closest penetrate at the same time. Of course there is no standard number really as it all depends on the tattooist.

Tattoo artists have to sharpen the needles on a stone after each use. This requires unwrapping the needles and rewrapping them with new thread before each session

"That can get really expensive using all that silk thread!" a tattooist confessed.

All tattoo artists have their own secret way they have adapted their needles, which they guard carefully along with all the other tools of their trade. So, since they are not prone to allowing people to view their preferred implements, I (Tamabayashi) decided to have myself tattooed. The second generation Horiuno (Real name Ginjiro1877-1958) could hardly refuse to show me his tools if I was going to be tattooed.

Tattooing Terminology

Tattoos are done by first deciding upon a plan, the outline of the main shape is done and then the tattoo is filled in. In the early Edo Period this was done by three different artisans, but by the end of that era professional tattoo artists took care of the entire process.

Kanji	Reading	Meaning
筋彫	Suji-bori	Outline tattoo of the main figures
羽彫	Hane-bori	Raising the end of the needles up after piercing, this allows more color to penetrate
隠彫	Kakushi-bori	Tattooing erotica, usually in a hidden area
ボカシ	Bokashi	Fill (no Kanji for this word)
毛彫	Ke-bori	Making fine, hair like lines
化粧彫	Kesho-bori	Tattooing filler items like Sakura, leaves, etc between main subjects
二重彫	Niju-bori	Tattooing tattoos on a figure in a tattoo
さらふ	Sarafu	Re-tattooing/ refreshing a tattoo
額	Gaku	Total shape of the tattoo. So named because the total shape of back tattoos in the old days looked like a rectangle with the corners cut off.

Bad Habits

There were some less than reputable tattoo artists out there. Some attempted to rush jobs, compressing a two hour tattoo into one hour. Others tried to make the process less painful by mixing cocaine into the ink.

Shapes

There are several different ways to finish the edge of a tattoo.

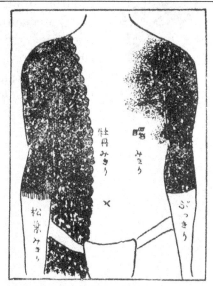

種四型のリキミ

Kanji	Reading	Illustration	Meaning
ぶっ切り	Bukkiri		Tattoo stops in a line. This is shown on the forearm (right side of illustration)
曙 みきり	Akebono Mikiri		"Dawn" the tattoo fades in/out (right side, chest)
牡丹 みきり	Botan Mikiri		The edge forms a repeating shape like peony flowers (left side, chest)
松葉 みきり	Matsuba Mikiri		The tattoo fades in with pine needle like lines (left forearm)

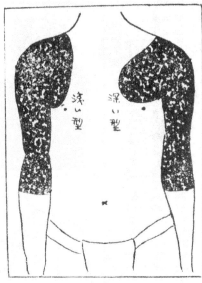

種二型のヘカヒ

Hikae
The front of the shoulder

There are two ways to handle the front of the shoulder, Asai Kata, or shallow style, which does not extend over the chest (left side of the illustration.) The Fukai Kata, or deep style, extends outward onto the front of the chest, past the nipple (right side of illustration.)

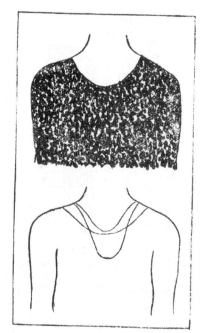

種三型のリグェ

Eguri
Neckline

The Eguri, or neckline can be handled in a few different ways.

Waki no Shita
Under the Arm

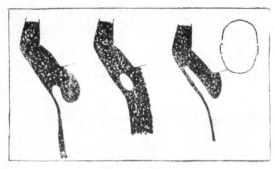

種 三 型 の 下 の 腋

Three ways to handle the area under the arm

There are some people that say the reason the area under the arm is left blank is to differentiate between prison tattoos but the real reason is because this area is particularly painful.

Ashi no Kata
Top of the legs

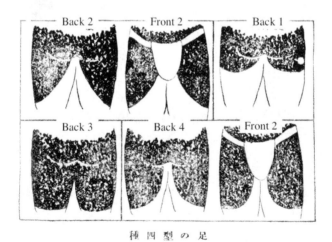

種 四 型 の 足

Four different ways to shape the leg tattooing.

Munewari
Chest Split

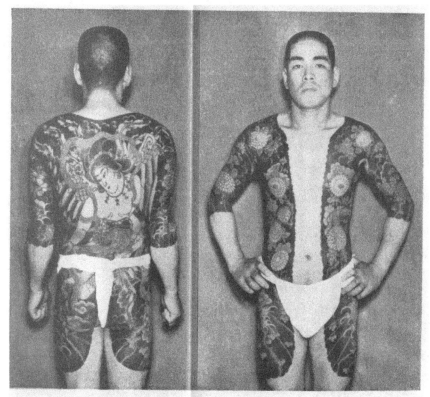

（しらちの菊は胸）女天作之宇彫目代二

Front and back picture of a tattoo done by the second generation Horimono-Shi Horiuno. The picture on the right shows the style of tattooing known as Munewari 胸割 "splitting the chest." The tattoos on the front are scattered chrysanthemums, on the back is a goddess. At first glance the sleeves of the tattoo seem to end with the above described Bukkiri style but, upon closer inspection they seem to be closer to Botan Mikiri.

Ink

Ink in general is called Sumi 墨. Japanese Ink is called Wazumi. Japanese ink is in solid blocks and is thinned out with water, rice water or Japanese Sake.

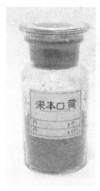

For colors 朱 Shu, or cinnabar is used. The powder was typically imported from China. The powder (picture, left) was mixed with animal glue from animal bone or skin. Cinnabar came in various colors, but the main ones were:

黄口 Koko – a rusty orange color
中口 Nakaguchi – an earthy yellow
赤口 Shakku - an earthy red

These colors were used by painters as well and are still in use today.

Benigara 紅殻 is a red made from vegetable oil, pine sap and pine soot that is very durable and resists fading in sunlight.

Purples, blues, greens and gold were achieved by making use of cosmetic powder.

Kobaien 古梅園"Aged Plum Garden"

Many tattoo artists in the Edo Era used ink from Kobaien, a calligraphy supply store in Nara. In particular the rectangular ink block branded as "Sakura" was the favored ingredient. One reason is to maintain consistency if a person got a tattoo from another tattoo artist. Therefore the tattoo artists all decided upon the Sakura ink block by Kobaien. Kobaien was founded in 1577 and is the oldest ink producer in Japan.

The image above is of a Sakura-zumi ink block for sale in the Kobaien shop. I contacted the shop, which is still in business, and the proprietor told me that a 65 gram block costs 4300¥, about 43$. Unfortunately they were unable to provide any additional information regarding the link to tattooing.

Old Ink Block

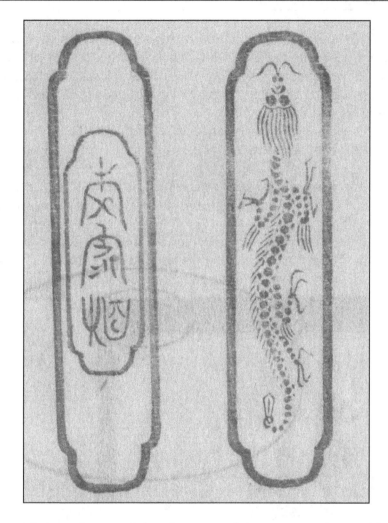

This is an image of the obverse and the reverse of an "Old Ink Stick" from a book written in 1795 called *A Small Record of Old Curios* 好古小録 by a dude named Toh Teikan 藤貞幹 1732-1797. It is part of the collection of Kofukuji Temple 興福寺 in Nara. It is said to have been made by a monk named Nitai 諦坊 who collected the soot from temple lanterns and mixed it with animal glue. The image of the dragon is particularly striking and seems to harken back to an earlier age. The dagger on the end of the tail may suggest it is an image of the Lord of Light Fudo transformed into a dragon.

Tattooing Apprenticeships

Those training to be tattoo artists first practice on Daikon radishes. The long radishes, which can be as thick as your wrist and around 50 cm long are dried for 3 days. This makes the surface taut. When practicing tattooing on the radish, not making the skin crack is a sign of progress.

The second generation tattoo artist Horiuno talked about his own training on radishes,

When I was in my apprenticeship I would get so into my training that I would go through 3 barrels of radishes in one sitting.

Moving onto tattooing people, the first subjects permitted would be simple masks on peoples arms like the Hyottoko mask. Then gradually apprentice "engravers" could move onto a single carp or a single Hannya devil mask.

Illustrations of various styles of Hyottoko masks. The word is written in Kanji as 火男 "fire man" because his mouth is puckered to blow onto a fire. He is often wearing a white and blue polka dot Tenugui scarf.

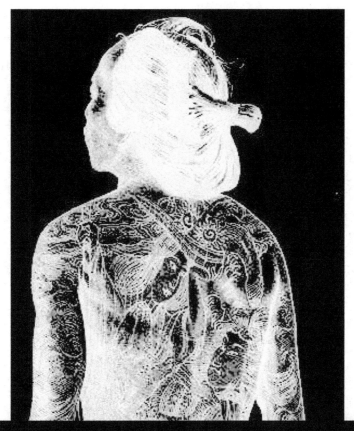

End of the Edo Era

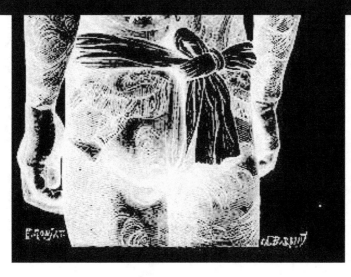

First Regulations

From the Meiwa Era up through the Kyowa Era (1764-1804) tattoos were, for the most part, self-applied, or done by a lover, or friend. In the following Bunka Era 1804-1818, tattoos becomes progressively more complicated and elaborate, and we see the emergence of professional tattoo artists. The placement of the tattoos also expanded, from the upper arm (a place easily concealed) to covering the arms, legs, chest and back. They even begin to cover the whole of the body. By the early to mid-1800s nearly all craftsmen, porters and other laborers were covered with full-body tattoos.

In the 8th year of Bunka, 1812 the government passed a regulation concerning tattoos. The order contains the following passage,

Of late some careless people have been displaying what is known as Horimono, carved designs or tattoos, on their flesh. They are carving various and sundry designs as well as words and such all over the body. The application of ink or coloring to the cuts is the problem at hand....Of late, there have also been a great number of those that perform this sort of carving seen about. Hereafter let it be known that clearly, carving tattoos, not only on the arms and legs, but also the rest of the body is inappropriate.

As the Bunsei Era 1818-1830 began, the tattooing being done became more and more dramatic and even attained a certain level of popularity. In the edition of the *The Fun Happy Laughing Reader* published in the 13th year of Bunsei it states,

The fashion of late seems to be to have illustrations tattooed all over the body to the extent one can hardly see the skin.

As the popularity of tattooing continued to increase the Bakufu government issued and distributed a ban on tattoos in August of the 13th year of Tenpo 1843. This was basically a repeat of the law that was issued in the 8th year of Bunka 1812 and the entire law is reproduced below:

People have been given to getting what is known as Horimono, or pictures or words engraved on various parts of the body. Ink or coloring is then applied. As there are those that are doing this, and it is not limited to those in the sex industry. In particular damaging an otherwise unblemished body with a scar is an embarrassment to yourself. Young people have begun to consider doing such things simply a matter of style. Though they may not realize they are being laughed at by a great many people. It is hardly a good thing that a great number of these kinds of people can be seen of late. It goes without saying that such a thing should not be done to the arms and legs, much less the entire body. The magistrates of the town should pay very, very close attention to this and detail how the thinking on tattooing is wholly misplaced.

Moreover to those that do the engraving described above, if a person should request such a thing to refuse it as a despicable and hateful thing would not be out of order. To continue to engrave as you like would be the mark of someone devoted to misconduct and insolence. Realize now that your mindset is completely wrong. Should a person come before you requesting a new engraving you should of course refuse the engraving and the application of ink. You should then state in no uncertain terms that this is something that is not to be done. Following that you should report such a person to the town magistrates. In particular the young people of each town should be lectured in no uncertain terms and without omission regarding each and all of the items mentioned above.

As the regulation indicates, receiving a tattoo or being involved in "engraving the flesh" as a profession is forbidden and punishable by a fine. For a time this succeeded in cooling the tradition of tattooing, however, the interval was short-lived and before long it was again being practiced at previous levels. In particular in the years spanning the Ansei and Manen Years 1854-1861, tattooed youths seeking to show off their bravery and make an impression would climb to the top of the towers over food shops and shout out greetings. Housewives and their children would see such grand displays of enthusiasm and actively seek out shops with such tattooed employees. It became fashionable for Geisha and Maiko to take lovers that had tattoos and it even became a source of pride.

Further, we cannot overlook the influence theater had on influencing the popularity of tattooing. Kabuki actors like Yoshinosuke and Denshichi Kyuro's who took on the role of the female mischief maker Benten Kozo, would roll up their sleeves to reveal dramatic tattooing at key moments in the performance. The beauty, power and strength demonstrated in that skin put people into a trance and it caused innumerable copycats.

Fake tattoos became popular toward the end of the Bakufu Era, paralleling the boom in tattooing. It consisted of painting colorful pictures on the skin to resemble tattoos. It was typically done with wax or oil based paints with color mixed in. If care was taken then they could be kept for three or four days. Amongst shopkeepers, Samurai and professional debauchers it enjoyed a brief popularity. Women working in the world of the Geisha would employ this method of temporary tattooing for festivals and other such occasions.

Illustration on following page: Japanese Tattooing by Augustus Henry (1833 – 1912).

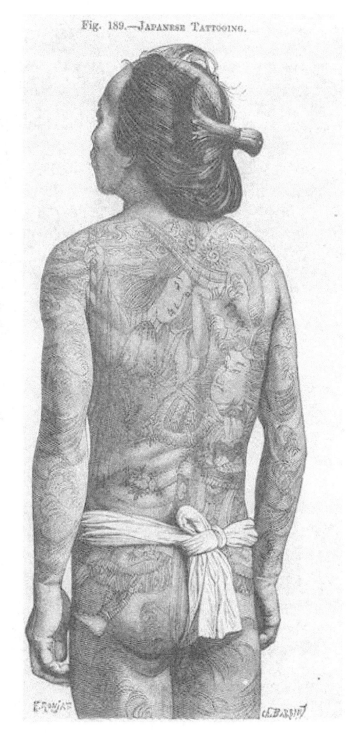

Fig. 189.—JAPANESE TATTOOING.

Tattoos as Punishment

Tattoos as Punishment Table of Contents
Tattooing as Punishment: Origins in China

Evidence for a tattooing culture in early China can be found in a number of texts that date from the mid-first millennium BCE to the nineteenth century CE.

In these texts at least six types of tattoo are mentioned:

1. Tattoos marking people different from the majority population
2. Tattoos as punishment
3. Tattoos of slaves
4. Tattoos in the military
5. Figurative tattoos
6. Textual tattoos

The courts in ancient China had five punishments for crimes. They were called the Five Punishments in the *Book of Documents* (possibly compiled by Confucius 551–479 BC). The Five Punishments 五刑 are:

1. 墨 Tattooing
2. 劓 Cutting off the nose
3. 刖 Cutting off the legs
4. 宮 Castration 去勢 for men, Confinement 幽閉 for women
5. 大辟 Death

The tradition of tattooing criminals was first carried out in the Shang dynasty in China around 1600 –1046 BC and is thought to have spread to Japan through the Korean peninsula.

Tattoo was considered a highly effective means of punishment in China for most of recorded history. Although we do not have verifiable information about pre- Zhou times, we can infer from texts written in the Zhou (1100-256 BCE) and the Han (206 -221 CE) that the tattooing or branding of criminals was probably widely used in ancient times as well as in dynasties possessing relatively reliable historical records.

-CE Reed *Early Chinese Tattoo* 2000.

The first four are mortification of the flesh in ascending order of severity with the final punishment being death. The penalties evolved and changed over time even in China.

In Japan the Taika Reforms were a set of doctrines established by Emperor Kōtoku in the year 645. They were written shortly after the death of Prince Shōtoku, and the defeat of the Soga clan, uniting Japan.

*It has been widely accepted that the character often used (in conjunction with others) for tattoo,*文 *wen in Chinese and Fumi or bun in Japanese meaning "to pattern" in fact was originally a representation of a person with a tattooed chest, and the other meanings of this character were derived from this original meaning.*
-Van Gulik, Irezumi

The oldest version of the Kanji 文, which means writing. The Kanji researcher Shirakawa Shizuka 白川静 theorized in his 1979 book *Ancient Culture of China* 中国古代の文化 that the oldest form of this Kanji depicts a person with a tattoo on their chest.

Early Edo Punishments

The following chart from the Edo Era gives an idea of the system in place. This chart is undated.

第十一章　五刑八虐六議及名例律　　〇節一刑名　大寶律ハ刑罰チ五トシ、各数等アリ、左ノ如シ	
死罪 〔二等〕 絞罪 斬罪	Death Level one: Strangulation (hanging) Level two: Death by sword
流罪 〔三等〕 近流 中流 遠流	Banishment Level one: Near 300 Ri (1,170 Kilometers) Level two: Middle 560 Ri (2,184 Kilometers) Level three: Far 1500 Ri (5,800 Kilometers)
徒罪 一年 一年半 二年 二年半 三年	Hard Labor Level one: One Year Level Two: 1.5 Years Level Three: 2 Years Level Four: 3 Years
杖罪 〔三等〕 六十 七十 八十 九十 百	Caning (Using 105 cm piece of bamboo with the joints shaved down) Level one: 60 Level Two:70 Level Three: 80 Level Four: 90 Level Five:100
笞 〔四等〕〔五等〕 十 二十 三十 四十 五十	Whipping Level one: 10 Level Two: 20 Level Three: 30 Level Four: 40 Level Five: 50

Late Edo Punishment

By the Late Edo (1800-1868) period the punishments were more varied. Some examples:

内容 crime	刑罰 punishment
尊属殺し patricide matricide	市中引廻しの上磔 Paraded around city and then crucified
主殺し killing your master	鋸引きの上磔 After being cut apart with a saw, crucified
辻斬り Killing a person to test a sword	引廻しの上死罪 Paraded around the city, decapitated
嘱託殺人 hiring a contract killer	下手人 Beheaded and your body used for test cutting swords
卑属殺し Killing your own flesh and blood	死罪～遠島 Death or Distant Banishment
地主、名主殺し Killing your landlord or local lord	市中引廻しの上獄門 Dragged through the city and beheaded with head displayed for 3 days
普通の殺人 Normal murder	下手人 Beheaded and your body used for test cutting swords
受託殺人 A contract killer	遠島～追放、重過料 Banishment or heavy fine
過失致死 Accidental death	死罪～遠島 Death penalty or banishment
正当防衛 Self-defense	相手方の親族、地主が赦免を願えば中追放 If the family pardons you, no crime

Tattoos as punishment: History in Japan

Since a tattoo cannot ever be erased, it was used a one kind of punishment. It was known as Geikei, or facial tattooing punishment, and also as Bokukei, or ink punishment. This was done in China from days long past and its influence reached to the ancient past of Japan. As was already mentioned the most easily visible portion of body, the face, was tattooed.

However up through the Kamakura Era the punishment of Rakuin 烙印, or branding was done. Whether this was done on the forehead or on the arm is not entirely clear, and may well have changed over time. The aftermath of this "punishment in the flesh" would leave the offender's face (or body) disfigured and the person could be easily identified as a prisoner. This punishment was used in favor of tattooing. However, the Edo period brought a resurgence to the method. This began with the fourth Tokugawa Shogun Ietsuna, who made it a part of his Kanbun Era 1661-1673 plan to govern Japan.

If a thief was sentenced to this punishment, then the criminal would have a Kanji tattooed on their forehead. However the eighth Tokugawa Shogun Yoshimune made it part of his policy in the fifth year of Kyoho 1716-1736 that thieves would have two fat lines tattooed on their arms. The actual regulation stated,

5th Year of Kyoho 1721. Irezumi : Two lines 9 mm wide should be tattooed on all prison inmates. This tattooed mark should be applied before they are released.

Other possibilities would be tattooing a ✚, X, ○, □, △, 麦 (the kanji for wheat,) the shape of a mountain, 卍(the symbol of Buddha) as well as others. Also the Kanji for dog 犬 could be tattooed onto the forehead. Typically this tattooing punishment would not be the main sentence but rather an additional punishment and it tended to be reserved for thieves. Amongst the general population it was known as Irezumi, or ink-punishment. The tattooing done by normal people was referred to as Horimono, or engraving, in Edo and Irebokuro, or placed mole, in Kyoto and Osaka.

In other words people verbally separated the type of tattooing done voluntarily and that done as a punishment.

The Encyclopedia of Old Laws

The Encyclopedia of Old Laws 古事類苑 (1896 to 1914) a Japanese encyclopaedic work initiated by the Meiji government, contains a detailed definition of Irezumi, tattooing.

Tattooing

Irezumi, or tattooing, is typically used after the original more, severe punishment for a crime has been reduced. During the time of Tokugawa Yoshimune, this punishment was often used in place of cutting off the nose or castration. The tattooing should be done at the prison. The room used for administration of this punishment should be about 10 paces across. The room should be set up as a sentencing chamber with seating arrangements for everyone. The inspector and the key holder take their places. The head prisoner leads the formation into the sentencing room. Hinnin, members of the lowest class a "non-person," accompany and assist the prisoner. The prisoner uncovers his left shoulder and arm. It is stabbed with a needle, ink is rubbed in and then he is put in a cell for three days.

When the tattoo has healed the prisoner is released. The shape of the tattoo differs from region to region. Most who are tattooed are also exiled from the city. If the person attempts to burn off or cut off the tattoo the tattoo will be re-applied in the same place. If so they will be permanently banished from Edo (Tokyo.)

The punishments of cutting off the nose and castration were carried out under the first Tokugawa Shogun but were abolished in the 6th year of Kanei 1629.

However, they were both re-instated in the 3rd year of Kyoho 1718. Tattooing as a punishment was established in the 5th year of Kyoho 1720. This punishment stayed around for a long time before being abolished. The punishments of branding and cutting off the finger (s) was only applied during the reign of the first Tokugawa. Following his reign it was abolished. Shaving the head was a punishment reserved for women for committing adultery. The head is shaved with a razor and the hair is presented to the parents.

入墨圖

牢屋附詰番
小傳馬町河岸
小屋頭
非人

同抱
有髪
非人

繩取
牢屋下男

The Encyclopedia of Old Laws contains the above illustration and description. The English translation of the text is below.

This is how the head of the Kodenma prison in Edo conducts tattooing. The tattooing is directed by the head prisoner, who is a Hinin (non-human.) Another Hinin prisoner, described as "having hair" (not shaved?) holds the one sentenced to tattooing. A Hinin (non-human) does the tattooing. The rope is held by another low level prisoner.

203

Illustration of the Official Tattooing Procedure (Japanese)

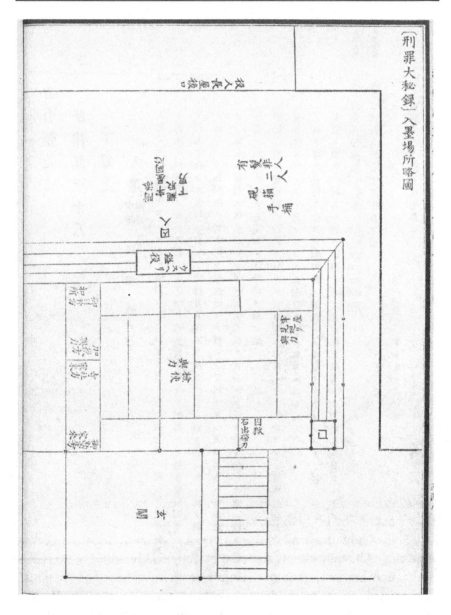

Illustration of the Official Tattooing Procedure (English)

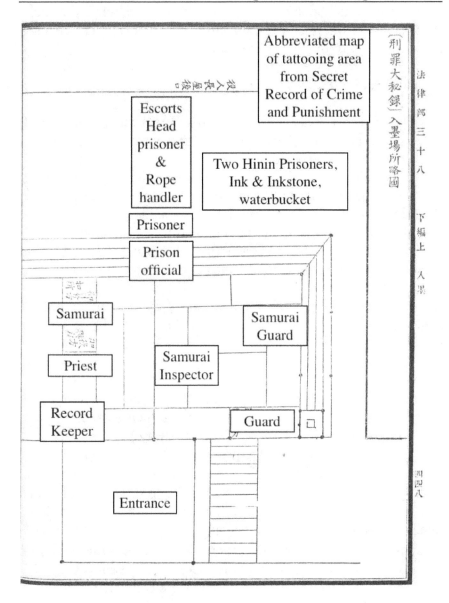

Abbreviated map of tattooing area from Secret Record of Crime and Punishment

Escorts Head prisoner & Rope handler

Two Hinin Prisoners, Ink & Inkstone, waterbucket

Prisoner

Prison official

Samurai

Samurai Guard

Priest

Samurai Inspector

Record Keeper

Guard

Entrance

The Secret Record of Crime and Punishment

This next section is from an anonymously written book called *The Secret Record of Crime and Punishment,* written around 1800. This section of the book details the process for tattooing a prisoner. It prescribes the number and status of the people in attendance and the responsibly of the main participants.

Instructions for Tattooing

The officer on duty is called forth and told that a sentence of tattooing has been passed and to bring forth the prisoner. The officer on duty goes to the cell and retrieves the prisoner, bringing him out with a rope tied around his waist. The rope is held by a low level prisoner. The prisoner to be tattooed and the prisoner holding the rope are escorted by a Dojin, civilian police assistant.

They should walk on the path around the designated building and stop at the front. A woven bamboo grass mat called a Mushiro should be spread on the ground. The prisoner should be made to sit on top of this mat.

On the veranda, which is raised above the ground about one meter, spread out a light green mat for the jailer. The prisoner's name along with his age and the date should be read out.

The prisoner's age is recorded (not date of birth, because everyone became a year older on January 1st. This is known as Kazoedoshi, counting years, and still plays a part in determining lucky and unlucky years for people based on their Kazoedoshi not their birthday which can be several months away.)

Next, the Hinin is instructed to proceed.

Note: Hinin 非人 was a social status that meant non-human. The lowest possible class of society. Some people were born into this class such as those that worked in "unclean" professions such as butchering animals, tanning hides and even street performers and prostitutes. Another name they were know by was Eta 穢多, an abundance of defilement. Executions were done by Hinin as was the handling of dead bodies. Other people were convicted of a crime and demoted to Hinin. In this case, a Hinin is summoned to do the tattooing.

Illustration of a member of the Eta caste preparing animal hides. From *Illustrated Guide to Workers of Edo*.

Instructions for Tattooing continued:

The prisoner opens his robe and frees his left arm. An inspection should be done to determine if the prisoner has any Horimono, engraving (tattooing), on his arm. Having done this a brush and ink is used to make a preliminary drawing on the prisoner's arm. Two lines are painted all the way around the arm. A bundle of needle is then used to engrave this into the prisoner's arm.

The Hinin then dips his finger in ink and spreads the black over the pricked surface. The Hinin should use both hands to massage the ink in. The bucket of water should be poured over the arm to wash the excess ink off. Then use Tenugui towel to wipe the area down. If the tattooing is insufficient, apply ink directly to the needle bunch and engrave any sections that are incomplete.

Having done this, again wash the area with water from the bucket and wipe it down with the Tenugui.

The prisoner should be marched over to where the head jailer is observing. This should be a Samurai of high rank, and he should be carrying a sword. The head jailer confirms that the tattoo is sufficiently dark and that two lines are encircling the arm. The tattooed arm should be wrapped with a paper bandage and the prisoner returned to his cell. He should be kept there for three days until the tattoo dries. Having determined that the tattoo has dried sufficiently the prisoner is called forth by a Samurai and release.

For the most part Edo police follow these procedures but in other regions there is some variation.

Legal Resources

The book *Legal Resources*, which covers the laws from the Edo Era up to the early 20th century, contains a chapter titled *How Tattooing Should Be Done*, that provides information on the tattooing process and detailed illustrations of how tattooing differs from region to region.

How Tattooing Should Be Done (Japanese)

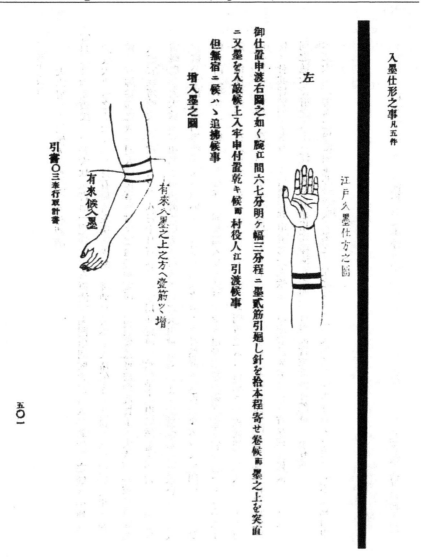

How Tattooing Should Be Done (English)   Edo Era

Illustration of tattooing done in Edo. This is the left hand. The punishment should be done as shown in the illustration on the right. Two bands should be tattooed around the arm. The lines should be about 1 cm thick with an interval of 1.8 – 2.1 cm between. (The interval is described as 6 -7 Bun, an archaic measuring system. 1 Bun is 3 millimeters.) For the tattoo tie together 10 needles into a bunch. After brushing on the ink use the needles. After engraving all the way around the arm, re-apply the ink. Keep the prisoner in his cell until the tattooing has dried. After that hand him over to the constabulary in their town. However, if they have no domicile then they should be banished.

For additional crimes another band is added below the original two.

Bokugu Tattooing Tools

This is called Irezumi Hari, or Tattooing Needle.

Note: The description of the tool used for tattooing is brief but the illustration at left illustrations give an idea of the kind of tool used. The image at left shows a rectangular box with needles. This doesn't quite match the description above of a bunch of needles tied together, however a box like this would probably make the process easier.

Punishment Tattoos By Region   **Edo Era**

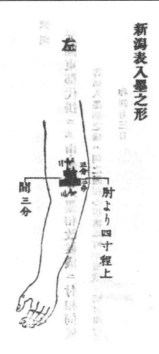

Niigata

This is an example of the tattooing done by the police department and prisons in Niigata. This is the tattoo performed by the police stations in Niigata after a prisoner is sentenced. The tattoo should be positioned about 12 cm above the elbow. The dimensions are below.

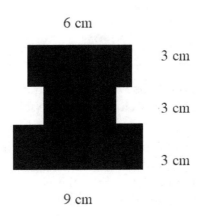

Kanto Area

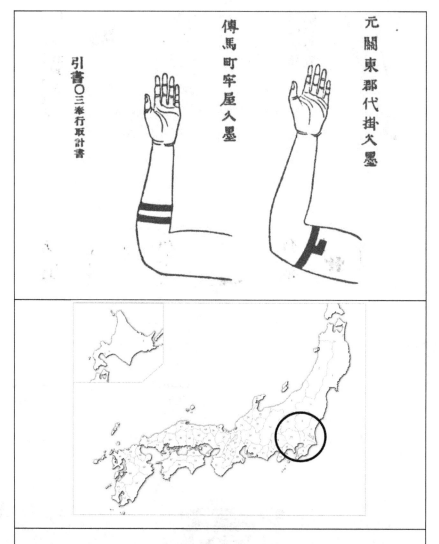

The above two tattoos were done in the Kanto area, roughly within the circle on the map above. The tattoo on the right was done throughout the Kanto area and resembles the Jutte 十手 police officer's iron truncheon, which had a hook that could be used to catch a sword blade.

The illustration on the right is the tattoo done by the police department in Denmacho prison in Edo.

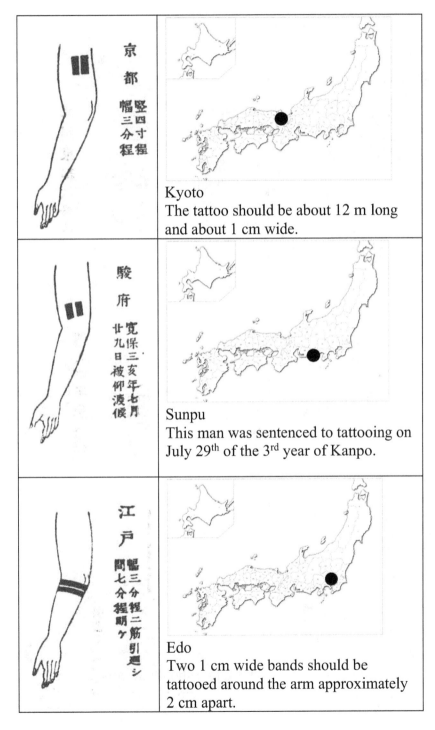

Kyoto
The tattoo should be about 12 m long and about 1 cm wide.

Sunpu
This man was sentenced to tattooing on July 29th of the 3rd year of Kanpo.

Edo
Two 1 cm wide bands should be tattooed around the arm approximately 2 cm apart.

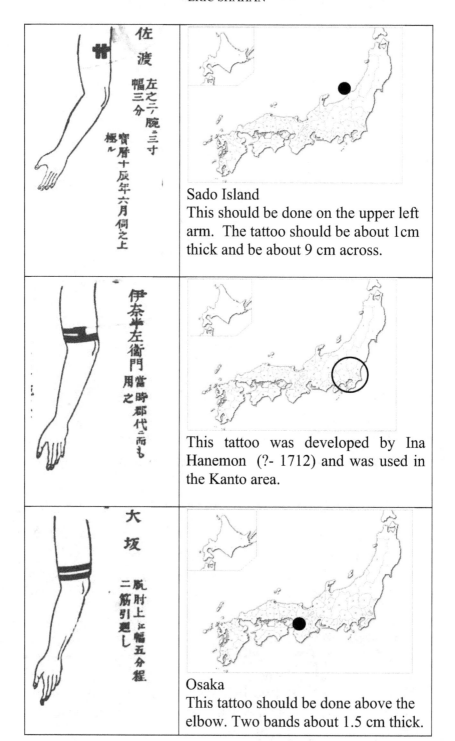

佐渡　左之二ノ腕二寸
幅三分
極ル　寶暦十辰年六月伺之上

Sado Island
This should be done on the upper left
arm. The tattoo should be about 1cm
thick and be about 9 cm across.

伊奈半左衛門　當時郡代ニ而も
用之

This tattoo was developed by Ina
Hanemon (?- 1712) and was used in
the Kanto area.

大坂　肱肘上ニ幅五分程
二筋引廻し

Osaka
This tattoo should be done above the
elbow. Two bands about 1.5 cm thick.

堺

候一寸程横ニ壹筋入墨

堺入墨之儀右腕肘より

寛延四未年四月十五日
山田伊豆守伺之上極ル

堀田相模守殿御下知

弾左衛門

左之腕肩先より三寸下竪ニ
入墨長二寸程幅三分程

寛保三亥年八月三日弾左衛門願之通申付墨込無宿
共欠落いたし候得ハ捕之入墨いたし候入墨二筋ニ
相成候上ハ死罪ニ相成ル

長崎

長一寸五分程手首より墨之間大方三分程
候出来物ニ簓も有之候得ハ右之方ニ可然
長崎麦入墨之候松浦河内守長崎奉行勤役之節ハ江戸
麦同様之入墨ニいたし候由

弾左衛門

盗之入墨

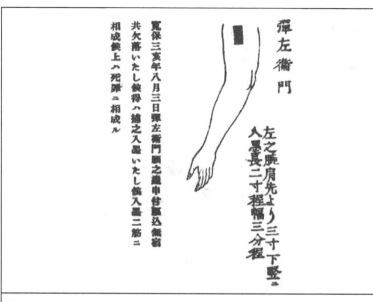

相成候上ハ死罪ニ相成ル

共欠落いたし候得ハ捕之入墨いたし候入墨二筋ニ

寛保三亥年八月三日弾左衛門願之通申付區込編容

弾左衛門

左之腕肩先より三寸下竪ニ
入墨長二寸程幅三分程

This tattoo should be done on the left arm. It should start 9 cm below the shoulder. The tattoo should be about 6 cm long and about 1 cm wide.

On August 3rd of the third year of Kanpo a man by the name of Dansaemon was given this tattoo. He was Kakeochi 駆け落ち which was a person who had left his community because of illegal activities and was now living on the run. The same term also applied to the homeless The was apprehended and tattooed. A second offence means that another tattooed stripe will be added. The third offence results in the death penalty.

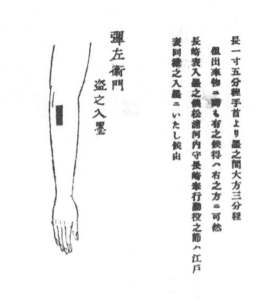

彈左衛門
盜之入墨

長一寸五分程手首より肘之間大方三分程
但出来物ニ罷も有之候得ハ右之方ニ可然
長崎表入墨之儀松浦河内守長崎奉行勤役之節ハ江戸
表同様之入墨ニいたし候由

This is the second tattoo given to Dansaemon. This one was for thievery.
Note: It is not clear if Dansaemon was eventually executed or that this is what would have happened if he committed another crime. Seems likely he got his head whacked off though.

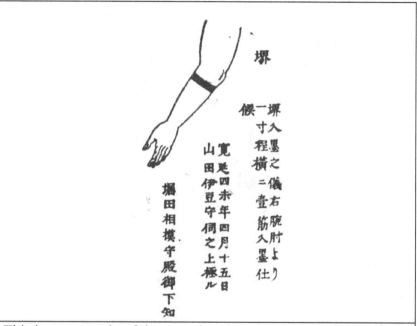

This is an example of the tattooing done in Kai? The tattooing starts about 3 cm below the elbbow. One band of tattooing is done.

Mr. Yamata, the Guardian of Izu, decided that thiswould be the offical tattooin On April 15th of the fourth year of Kanen.

Lord Horita the Guardian of Soma gave his consent.

Note: Despite the fact that they seem to be high ranked Samurai, I could not find any information about these people.

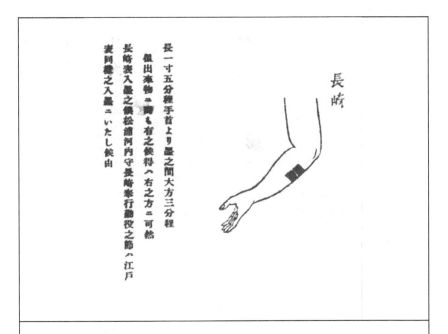

長崎

長一寸五分程手首より肱之間大方三分程

佃出来物ニ蒲も有之候得ハ右之方ニ可然

長崎表入墨之候松浦河内守長崎奉行勤役之節ハ江戸

表阿蘭陀之入墨ニいたし候由

Nagasaki

The tattooing should be above the wrist and about 4 cm long.
The interval between the stripes should be about 9 cm.

There will be some differences in tattooing so the illustration at right should be thought of as an example.

This is the Irezumi Punishment used in Nagasaki. Mr. Matsuura, the Guardian of Kawauchi, instituted this practice. The police in Edo also began using this tattoo.

Note: This section partially illegible.

Punishment Tattoos By Region: 2

This section only lists the area with arm illustrations.

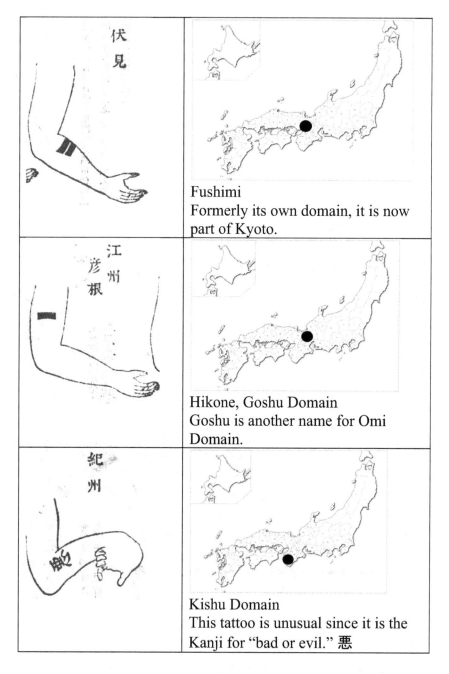

Fushimi
Formerly its own domain, it is now part of Kyoto.

Hikone, Goshu Domain
Goshu is another name for Omi Domain.

Kishu Domain
This tattoo is unusual since it is the Kanji for "bad or evil." 悪

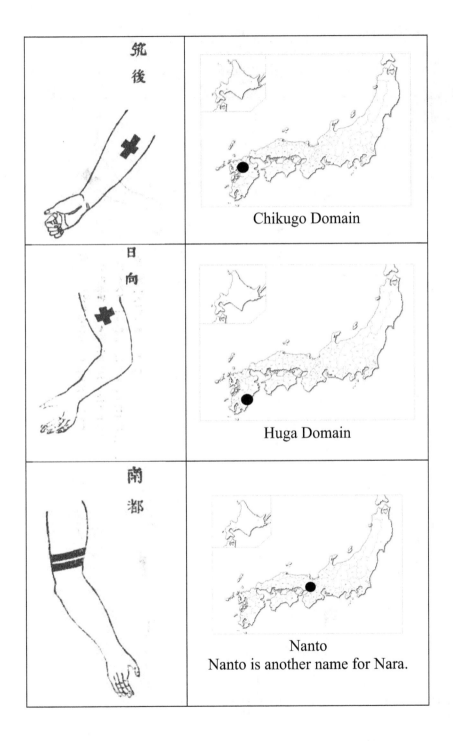

筑後

Chikugo Domain

日向

Huga Domain

南都

Nanto
Nanto is another name for Nara.

Punishment Tattoos By Region: 3

This section includes facial tattooing along with the region.

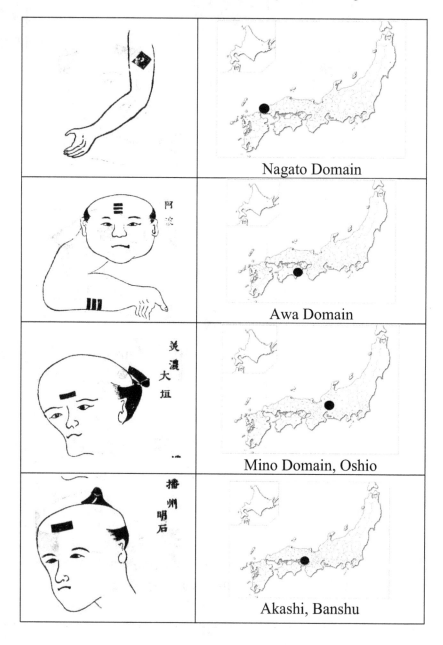

Nagato Domain

Awa Domain

Mino Domain, Oshio

Akashi, Banshu

Punishment Tattoos By Region: 4

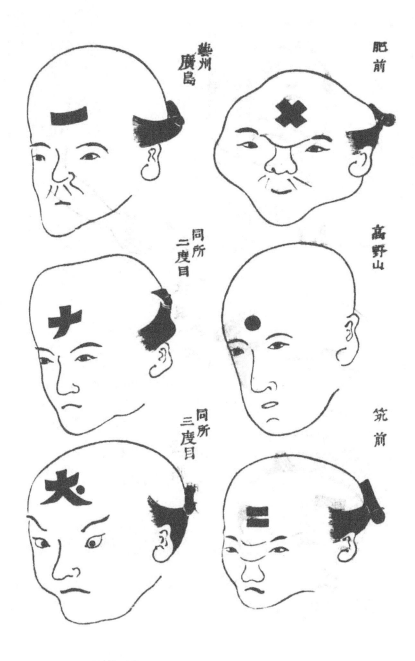

Hiroshima
First offence

Hiroshima
Second Offence

Hiroshima
Third offence

Adding the final stroke and dot makes the Kanji for dog. In this era, dogs were considered a lowly animal in Japan. The standard Kanji for dog is below. The Kanji for dog in the illustration at left is probably a local variant.

犬

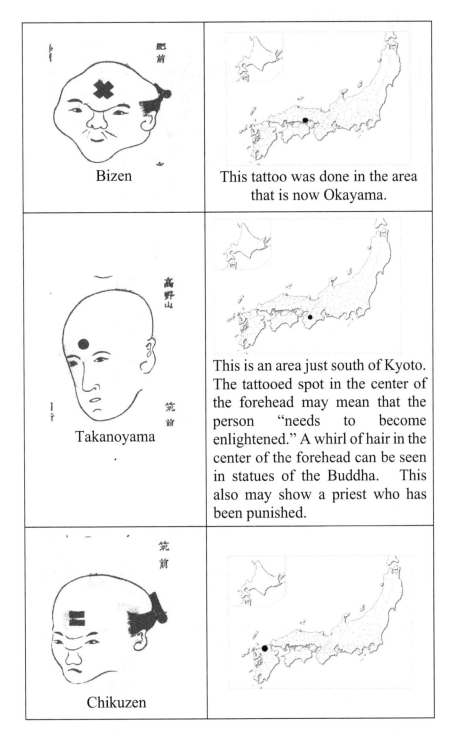

Bizen	This tattoo was done in the area that is now Okayama.
Takanoyama	This is an area just south of Kyoto. The tattooed spot in the center of the forehead may mean that the person "needs to become enlightened." A whirl of hair in the center of the forehead can be seen in statues of the Buddha. This also may show a priest who has been punished.
Chikuzen	

Punishment Tattoos By Region: 4

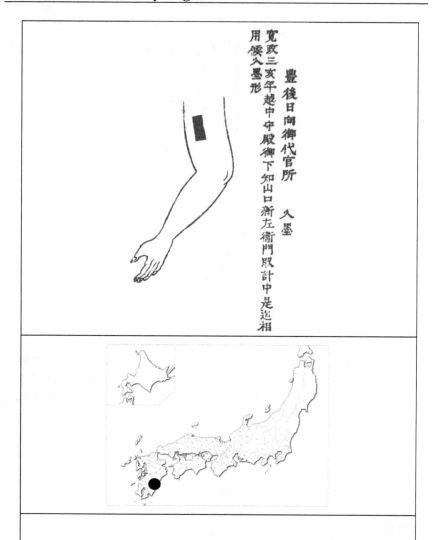

This is the tattoo used by the police in the Bungo and Hyuga areas of Kyushu.

In the 3rd year of Kasei 1782, by the order of the Guardian of Echicu Yamaguchi Shinsaemon was tattooed with this mark.

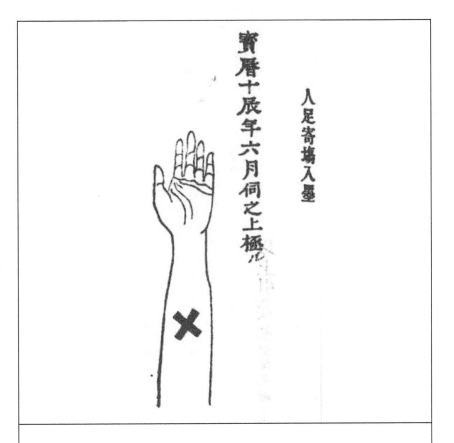

This is a tattoo used at the Reformatory 加役方人足寄場 かやくかたにんそくよせば a training center for the unemployed, homeless or those convicted of a petty crime. It was located in Edo roughly where the Tsukiji fish market is today. It is estimated that 300-400 men were in the facility at any one time. The facility was set up in 1790 with the goal of reforming petty criminals and homeless by teaching them a trade. It was closed in 1868. It is not clear if all the men sent to this facility had this tattoo or this was a penalty.

This man was tattooed in June of the 10th year of Horeki 1761.

Also, it is not clear why the tattoo is in 1761 but the facility was set up in 1790.

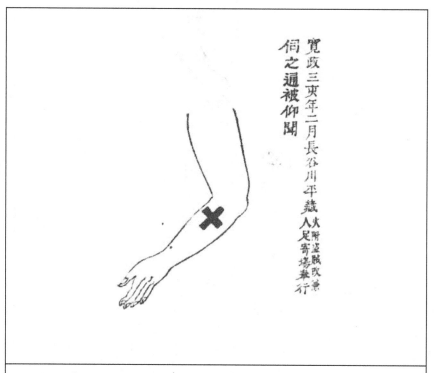

In February of the 3rd Year of Kansei Hasegawa Heizo used this mark for those sent to the Reformatory.

Note: Hasegawa (1754 – 1795) was a police officer originally from Kyoto and later assigned to Edo. He was famous for being a bit of a troublemaker in his youth but later steadily climbed the ranks as a police officer. He was famous for being tough but fair and founded the Reformatory in Ishikawa Island as a way to re-integrate people back into society.

His exploits were fictionalized by the author Ikenami Shotaro 池波 正太郎 (1923 –1990.) The series of historical novels he wrote featuring Hazegawa Heizo were called The Crime Journal of the Devil Detective 鬼平犯科帳, which later became a television series, a manga and anime.

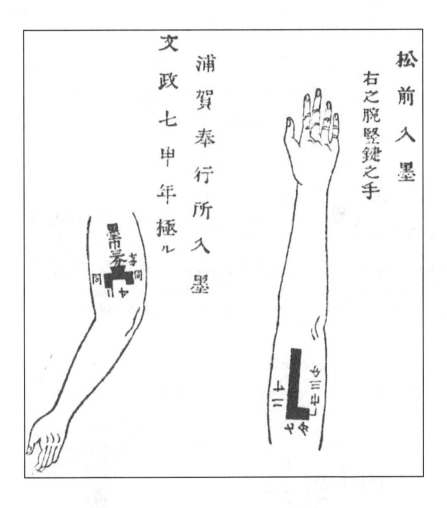

松前入墨

右之腕竪鍵之手

浦賀奉行所入墨

文政七申年極ル

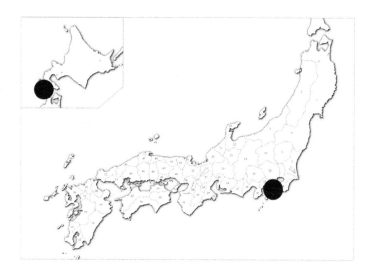

Left: Uraga city (map lower right)
This is the type of tattooing done by the police in Uraga Domain in the 7th Year of Bunsei, 1825.

Right: The Matsumae Domain in the northern Hokkaido Island. This tattoo was done on the right arm and resembles the key (probably referring to the hook on the end of a Jutte police officer's truncheon.)

Below: Dimensions of the tattoos.

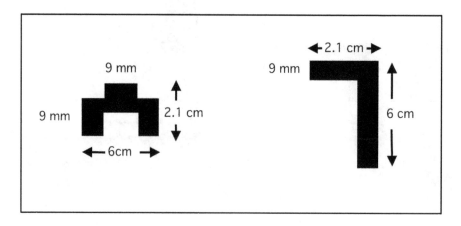

O-Sadamegaki 1

O-sadamegaki 御定書 are regulations by either the central Bakufu government or a local government. They are bound into books and are kind of a book of laws. They sometimes contain information on punishment tattoos.

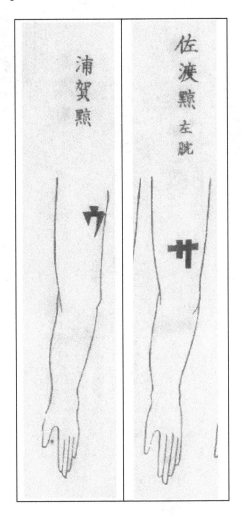

The illustration on the left is from Uraga. The one on the right is from Sado Island. These regions use the Katakana alphabet to tattoo prisoners. Uraga tattoos ウ, which is the first letter/sound in the name ウラガ. Sado Island does the same with サ.

O-Sadamegaki 2

This is another version of the previous illustrations done on a single page.

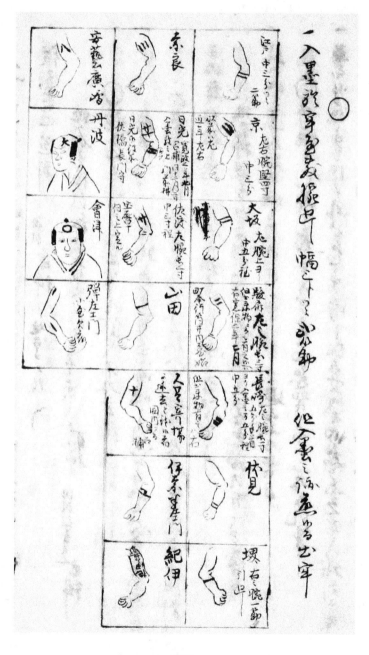

Ando or Hiro	Nara	Edo
Tanba	Nikko	Kyoto
Aizu	Sado Island	Osaka
Dansaemon	Yamata	Shunpu
	Reformatory	Fushimi
	The arm of Ina Hanemon	Fushimi
	Kii domain	Kai Domain

An Illustrated Guide to Tokugawa Bakufu Policing

This is an interesting resource that is not only illustrated but has a few English descriptions. *An Illustrated Guide to Tokugawa Bakufu Policing* 徳川幕府刑事図譜 edited by Fujita Shintaro藤田新太郎 1893. I have only presented the sections that deal with tattooing though this book is an overview of the Tokugawa crime and punishment system.

PREFECE.

Since a revolution of the first year of Meidi (1863) Japan had changed all the conditions of state, and is now at the wonder ful Progress of civilization, so that it is administrated by the constitutional goverment. Long before the revolution Japan was governed by a Despotism of shoguns or Taikuns. The punishments of this time were very creul, so as indicated by this picturebook. No longer Japanese almost memory these creulties, and therefore this has now become one of japanese history. The book is divided into three parts, each containing a blief explanation: 1. Commiting the crims, 2 old Punishments by shoguns, which are the plincipal subject of this work, 3 Justices of our time: On compariny these facts you will understand how Japan is presently changing and civilizating its state·

June 10, the 26 year of Meidi(1893)

Author.

刺青仕置の圖

The punishment of tattooing by native tattooers on the skin of some native culprit. I was informed by our guide that the man was more tenacious of, and rather fancied, every grievous punishment should be exerted on him.

Illustration of Tattoos as Punishment

English text under the illustration is a little convoluted, so here is a contemporary translation:

Tattooing is done as punishment. Ink is pushed into the skin with a needle. Anyone seeing this tattoo will understand that he is a criminal. If he is caught again the punishment will be more severe.

It is interesting to note that this book does not state that those doing the tattooing are all prisoners and non-human Hinin. It does show the rope tied around the waist and the Irezumi Hari, or tattooing needles. The person applying the tattoo also has a brush in his hand and has clearly first painted the ink on the arm before beginning to prick it with the needle.

Illustrations of Tattooing

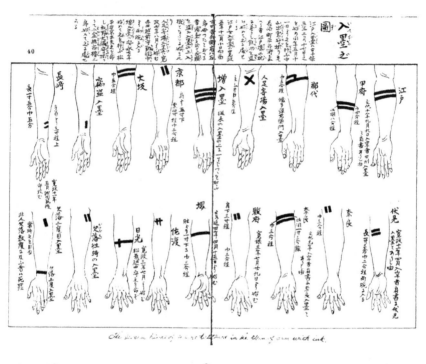

One given kind of is one tattooed in the skin of arm with ink.

Text:

Illustrations of the different kinds of tattoos used on criminals.

This illustration shows how the tattoos differ from region to region, but they are the same as the ones previously mentioned.

Illustration of Tattooing

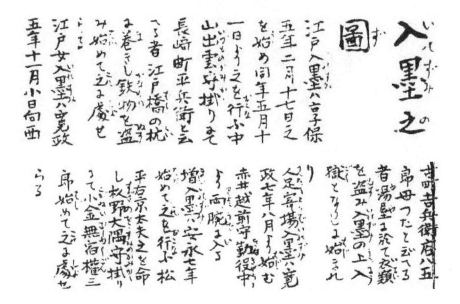

Translation of Text:

This Edo Period Irezumi, or tattooing, was done on February 17th of the 5th year of Kyoho, 1720. On May 11th of the same year, tattooing as punishment began to be carried out. The first time it was applied was by Nakayama the Guardian of Izumo Domain. He sentenced a man known as Hirabe of Nagasaki Town tattooed for, amongst other things, stealing the metal around the footing of a bridge in Edo.

The first woman to be tattooed occurred in November of 1720. It occurred in West Old Town of Huga Domain. The mother of Yoshi Hyoei, known as Mama Goro, stole clothing from a shop called Yuya. She was tattooed and thrown in the slammer.

The policy of tattooing those sent to the Reformatory began in February of the 7th year of Kansei. When Mr. Akai, the Guardian of Echizen, was in charge the policy of tattooing both arms began.

The adding of additional tattooing began in the seventh year of Anei. This was ordered by Matsudaira Ukyo Taifu. It was first carried out by Sugino the Guardian of Osumi on a man named Gonsaburo who was having money trouble and had no domicile.

Ten Case Studies from *Selected Examples of Sentencing*

刑例抜萃
Selected Examples of Sentencing
Edited by Ohashi Yosaemon
1810

The following examples are from a compilation gathered by Arson and Thievery Rectifier (Police Officer) Ohayashi Yosaemon. It was compiled in September of 1810. It was intended to serve as a sentencing guide.

The book collects 969 cases and records the crime, circumstances and punishment. It is divided into 22 books with a two-volume table of contents. Interesting the volumes are, for the most part, divided by punishment, not the crime. A sample of the chapter headings are,

- Burning at the Stake
- Crucifixion
- Beheading
- Tattooing
- 50 or 100 Lashes
- Letters of Apology

It also discusses handing of certain types/ classes of people including separate sections for minors, women, holy men and members of Samurai households. There is an entire volume just on criminals sentenced to tattooing, though there tattooing does appear in other volumes, usually in addition to other punishment.

Here are ten cases regarding tattooing recorded in this book.

1. November 4th of Kansei 9 1797

Recorded by Ideda under the Auspices of Lord Toda

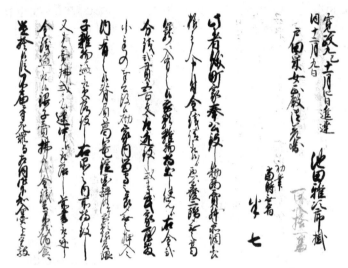

Handwritten text from the *Selected Examples of Sentencing*

Subject:
Hanshichi "Half-seven"
No known address.

What the police have been able to determine is that Hanshichi, disguised himself as a merchant in order to obtain money and a lot of dishonest things followed. He broke into a locked storage room on the second floor of a shop and stole clothing and small items. He also made off with 2 gold half-Ryo coins and 1500 Bun in small coin.

In addition, a man from a house owned by a Samurai reported to the police that Half-seven picked the lock on the storage house and snuck in while everyone was out. He stole clothes, a Wakizashi short-sword, silver talents and other assorted items. In addition, he sold some of these items.

When he was finally captured the above-mentioned items had all been sold and he had used all the money on alcohol and food.

For these crimes he was sentenced to death, but it was ameliorated, and he was given 100 lashes and tattooed.

The Tatakikei 敲き刑 or beating punishment was done with a kind of half whip half stick called the end of a broom 箒尻. It was about 60 cm long and about 9cm in diameter. The core was bamboo split into several sections, then wrapped with hemp paper and then bound with Kanzeyori 観世捻, a kind of paper string. Sometimes leather was wrapped around the handle.

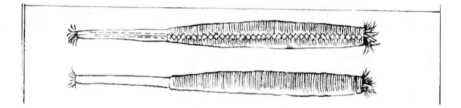

Illustration of a Chida or Muchiuchi used for beatings.

The caning and whipping were eventually combined into one punishment known as "beating" and the sentence was either 50 strikes for a "beating" or 100 strikes for a "severe beating."

Illustration of the Tatakikei being carried out. Strikes were done on the back arms legs and buttocks. Edo Era.

2. May 19th of Kansei 10 1798

Recorded by Ideda under the Auspices of Lord Ando

Illustration of men carrying rice bales from Hokusai's Sketchbook by Katsushika Hokusai. 1814.

Subject:
Hirakichi
No known address, but seen about the Kazusa area

Hirakichi made a habit of breaking holes in the walls of average people's houses and then ripping open the bales of rice and grains. He then either disposed of it (ate it?) or sold it. He was found in possession of items he had bought with the money he got from the stolen produce. The rest of the money he spent on alcohol and food.

He was given a severe beating and tattooed.

3. September 27th of Kansei 10 1720

Recorded by Ieda under the Auspices of Lord Toda

Citizens fleeing the Meireki fire of 1657. It is estimated 100,000 people died in this fire. Illustration from Record of Musashi 武蔵鐙 by Asai Ryoi 浅井了意(?- 1691)

Subject:
Kumaji "Next Bear"
No known address

 This man was hired to help clean up the debris after a Samurai family house had burned down. While he was sweeping up the ashes, he picked up the lid to a silver Sake serving bottle. He then took it home and sold it. He used all the money on food and alcohol.
 He was sentenced to tattooing and a severe beating but this last was ameliorated to just a regular beating.

4. March 26th of the 1st year of Bunka 1804

Recorded by Mamiya under the Auspices of Lord Toda

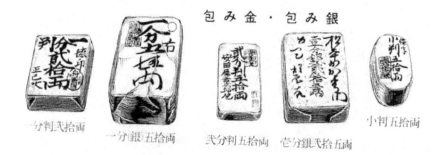

包み金 ・ 包み銀

一分判弐拾両   一分(銀)五拾両   弐分判五拾両   壱分銀弐拾五両   小判五拾両

Illustration of different gold and silver coins wrapped in paper with officially stamped amounts. The coins were bundled for easy payment of larger amounts.
From left to right: 20 Ryo in gold, 50 Ryo in silver, 50 Ryo in gold, 20 Ryo in silver, 50 Ryo in gold

Subject:
Norimichi
No known address

Norimichi was lurking around the temple and eventually found a way in through the kitchen door. He entered without anyone's permission. Making his way through the building he entered the living room and stole a stack of coins wrapped in paper. (This may have been an offering at the temple.) He was discovered on his way out. He fled at the sound of shouting and dropped the bundle of money.

He was tattooed and given a severe beating.

5. December 12th of the 7th year of Bunka, 1811.

Recorded by Ohayashi under the auspices of Lord Aoyama

A Nagamochi chest from the early 20th century.

Subject:
Tarokichi
No known address

This man broke into several houses of ordinary citizens. It appears he managed to get the doors open and sneak in. He then found keys to the portable Nagamochi dresser hidden in a comb case. He uses the key to open the Nagamochi. In addition, he went into the yard and absconded with clothing, belts, coins and other small items.

Later, camped at an illegal camp in an unnamed field behind Oiso hotel. There he gambled away 60 or 70 coins. They used dice and cups (this is probably the Chohan "even or odd game" described earlier.) It seems he initially won but began to trade the clothing he stole for more money.

When he was found Tarokichi was wearing some of the clothes in question. The rest he claims he threw away, pawned or sold. Since, neither the items nor the money could be reclaimed from Tarokichi he was sentenced to tattooing and a severe beating. However, upon further consideration that sentence was changed, and he was executed.

6. August 26th of the 4th year of Bunka 1808

Recorded by Arao under the auspices of Lord Makino

Subject:
Hirazo
Domicile Unknown place in Shimosa
Previously arrested for vagrancy

Hirazo was previously tattooed and given a severe beating. Following that he was sent to the Reformatory in Kamiro Village in Joshu, however he escaped. During his escaped he committed theft. He entered a peasant's house through the door, by some means. Sneaking in he stole clothing including a Haori jacket which he pawned or sold. He was eventually re-arrested and was in the process of being returned when, despite being tied up, he escaped again.

Along with several accomplices of the same ilk, Hirazo he robbed the houses of elderly, shops, Samurai households along with farmers and everyday citizens. They climbed over bamboo fences and walls alike, broke open doors and pushed their way in. All told they broke into six residences and stole items such as clothing, dry goods, belts, raincoats, mosquito netting and other items. The group then divided the items up amongst themselves and pawned, sold or passed the items on to others.

In addition, they also grabbed and threatened Iku, the wife of Tomigoro, telling her they would kill her husband and parents if she did not co-operate and allow them to leave unobstructed. After they left, they continued to make lewd comments to young women and mothers.

Upon being informed of the assault on Iku, assistant policeman Saemon was able to apprehend Hirazo. He was charged with indecent behavior and sentenced to being paraded around town, publicly executed and having his body used for test cutting while his head was mounted for viewing for three days. However, this was ameliorated to being paraded around town and decapitated with no subsequent display or use of the body.

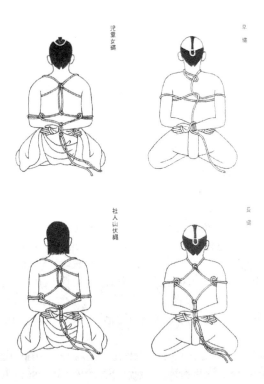

Hojo Jutsu, restraining techniques from Shinkage Shinnuki School. Illustration by Fujita Seiko. Clockwise from the top right: Rapid Restraining (with a short rope), Full Restraint, Restraint for monk or mountain acetic, restraint for women or children.

7. December 3rd of the 3rd year of Bunka 1807

Recorded by Arao the Guardian of Tanma
Under the auspices of Lord Makino the Guardian of Bizen

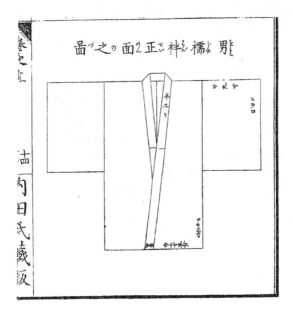

Illustration of a Juban undershirt from Sewing Manual for Girls 裁縫教授書：女学生徒 by Kubota Ryozan 久保田梁山 1878.

Subject:
Tsuma (female, from the section Female Offenders Section)

This incident occurred after Tsuma had set out on a pilgrimage to all the domains of Japan with her mother and older brother. Along the way she got separated from them and subsequently got engaged to a man by the name of Yoshigoro. However, it seems that continuing their relationship proved difficult so they ended their marriage.

Later, she entered the service of a man named Ihyoei. She then began an indecent relationship with Sadajiro, one of the men staying with Ihyoei.

Tsuma agreed to move in with Sadajiro, however as he had not stipend the two concocted a plan to steal in order to pay for their new life.

They stole Yoshigoro's Juban undershirt and pawned it. In addition, they covered their tracks by forging an entry into Ihyoei's log book under pawned items.

That same night she and Sadajiro agreed on a plan. While the master was out Tsume stole clothes, belts, a short sword, mosquito netting , scissors and coins. She then passed these items to Sadajiro.

He then sold these items to obtain funds. In addition, he used the aforementioned logbook of pawed items to collect further monies. As the pair was moving from place to place conducting these activities she got separated from Sadajiro.

While inquiring after the whereabouts of her mother and elder brother she sold off a few remaining items. She later ran into her brother and told him all that had happened but swore him to secrecy.

Though Tsuma was betrothed the relationship had been ended. Many items were lost and those affected applied for justice. Therefore she was tattooed an placed in solitary confinement for 50 days.

Note:

I don't often laugh whilst translating but this one cracked me up. They pawned his underpants! It sounds like the mother and brother set out on a pilgrimage to get Tsuma away from some earlier trouble, but she gave them the slip. Entries like this one are why the writer of the series the *Crime Logbook of the Devil Detective* used these incidents as a resource for his stories.

There are some interesting details such as the "pawned items logbook" which shows that Samurai were often short of money and relied on "lowly merchants" for cash infusions from time to time.

I think if Tsuma had still been married/betrothed she would not have been punished as severely. In all likelihood the husband would have had to take responsibility. Also, though it doesn't state explicitly, I think the brother turned her in. Probably sick of all her bullshit.

8. November 2nd of the 10th year of Kansei

Recorded by Ikeda Masajiro
Under the auspices of Lord Toda

Subject:
Yoshigoro
No known address, but from the Itabashi section of Edo
13 Years old (This is from the Young Offenders/ Under 15 years of age Section)

Yoshigoro was arrested for several crimes. While staying at the house of a friend he stole some coins. He also broke into several houses in town. In addition, he snuck into bathhouses and bathed without paying. Later he stole the clothing and personal items of other customers. He also broke into a place (a temple or shrine?) and made off with the offering box. He broke the box open and stole the coins. Most of the aforementioned items including the offering box and clothing were damaged lost or pawned. He also spent all the money he received from pawning the stolen goods.

He was sentenced to tattooing and 100 lashes with a cane but due to being under the age of 15 he was only tattooed.

9. April 7th of the 11th year of Kansei

Recorded by Ikeda Masajiro
Under the auspices of Lord Ando the Guardian of Taima

Ashigaru "light foot" low level Samurai and his assistant on the road to battle. Edo Era.

Subject:
Ito Naosaku
A former member of a Samurai household, now no known address

This man previously served as an Ashigaru (low level Samurai). He worked diligently and was given a place to stay at the home.

He entered (without permission) into an unlocked room on the second floor. From that room he took clothing, gold and silver pieces and assorted dry goods.

When arrested he had some of the articles of clothing and dry goods in his possession, but he spent some of the money on clothing for himself and lent some to others. The remaining money was used to buy alcohol and food at restaurants.

He neglected his duty as a Samurai to serve his household. He was sentenced to tattooing and 50 lashes with a cane but this was increased to tattooing and 100 lashes with a cane.

10. September 13th of the 1st year of Kyowa 1801

Recorded by Okabe Naiki
Under the auspices of Lord Toda

View down Shinyoshiwara in Edo. The houses on both sides are Machiya, residence-businesses. From *Illustrated View of Edo Life* 江戸風俗浮世絵大鑑 1917. Okubo Beisai 久保田米斎 1874-1937

Subject: Kiyotsugu
No known address but from Reigan "Ghost Shore" Island in Edo

Kiyotsugu was arrested for breaking and entering. He scaled a fence on the side of a Machiya. From there he made his way onto the roof. He broke open the window sash on the second floor and entered the residence. He was also found to have entered through the front door of some other houses. Kiotsugu entered vacant lots. He made off with clothes, mosquito netting and umbrellas that were hanging out to dry. Some of these items he kept for himself while others he destroyed and threw away or sold. None of the money from these sales remained.

Due to this unconscionable behavior he was sentenced to tattooing and 100 lashes with a cane.

First Hand Account

The earliest first-hand account of tattooing I could find was in a magazine called *Research Into Manners & Customs*. Over the course of two issues the author Ema Tsutomu introduces a man by the name of Kitazaki Genjiro, who he dubs "the most tattooed man in the world." The articles in question were published in the April and October 1934 issues of the magazine.

入墨：昔の入墨師
Tattooing: How Tattoo Artists Used to Work
By Ema Tsutomu 江馬務

I gave a lecture on tattooing in February (1934) in Osaka. After my lecture I introduced Mr. Kitazaki Genjiro who is a special patient at Osaka Imperial University of Medicine. He then stripped naked and showed his body, which had been completely tattooed over the course of six years. The crowd of people who attended the lecture, well over a hundred strong, gave an audible gasp. Since the explanation of tattooing he gave was a true story, it was an extremely rare and informative experience.

Mr. Kitazaki talked about what inspired him to get himself tattooed and the answer was, that though he took the test to become a soldier in the imperial arm, he failed to meet the standard required. He petitioned to re-apply, but was denied. In a fit of rage and a desire for self-destruction he got himself tattooed.

Having his entire body tattooed took six or seven years and cost around 300¥. When asked about the benefits of being tattooed he responded with,

One day I watched as a certain British Battleship came into Osaka Port. Some of the sailors saw my tattoos and were so impressed they took me out to dinner. The same thing happened to me in Kyoto. A certain rather well-known person invited me to his house and treated me quite grandly. That sort of thing happens a lot, getting taken out for a feast as a special guest. Recently, I've been invited to work at a medical school because of my tattoos.

Mr. Kitazaki also said that working at the hospital means, if he becomes sick, all the doctors work hard to help him.

In response to the question, "Are there any downsides to having tattoos?" he responded,

Before I got tattooed people would sometimes ask me to settle disputes. Afterword's, they would both have to take me out to dinner. Then, laughing, he added, *That doesn't happen anymore!*

Next I asked him, "What was the most painful place to get tattooed?" In response to this he said, "My stomach."

He ended the talk by saying,

The other day I caught a cold and went to see the doctor to get a shot. He asked me how much it hurt to get all my tattoos done and I replied, "Is looking at my tattooing making you want to get one?!" The doctor and I both had a good laugh at that.

入墨経験談
My Experience Getting Tattooed
By Kitazaki Genjiro 北崎源次郎
"The Most Tattooed Man in the World"

My name is Kitazaki Genjiro and I have been asked to talk about my experience with tattooing. (Born in 1874 in the Sakai area of Osaka.) The reason I decided have myself tattooed is because I failed the recruitment test for the Imperial Army (In 1895 at the age of 21 he was declined for military service due to being less than the minimum height of 154 cm.) Due to that I fell into a rage and depression. My outlook was bleak so I accepted an invitation from my friend who was a Yakuza member. Because I started slowly and only got work done infrequently it took 6~7 years to complete. As to the question of how much it cost, I would have to say roughly 300¥, or about 3000¥ in today's (1934) money (Now this would be roughly 50~60,000$.)

Later, I received an invitation from Osaka Medical School. The substance of the offer was after my departure from this mortal coil my skin would be peeled off an attached to a life sized model of my body. My bones would be leaned and preserved while my organs would be removed and placed in jars for permanent preservation. I don't think there is any greater honor than this. And it is all due to my tattooing. Currently, I am employed at the Osaka Imperial University. If I ever become sick, the medical professionals all work very hard to treat me. A lot of them are interested in me because they want to see if there is a connection between a tattooed body and illness.

The day I agreed to donate my body to Osaka Hospital was October 9th of Meiji 42 (1909.) As you all know the Imperial date of 42 and the month 10 and the day 9 can be read as Shi・Ni・To・Ku which is a homophone for A Grand Day to Die. Truly auspicious! That being said, I'm no big fan of dying!

When tattooing, bundles of the needles used for sewing silk are used. These are in bunches of 5, 15, 30 or 45 needle, but the one that really hurts is the 80 needle bunch. This is what they look like (At this point Mr. Kitazaki shows some needles.) They pierce around 2.4 to 3mm below the skin. A short brush with the hair on the end trimmed short is used. This brush is held by two fingers of the left hand. The right hand holds the needles, and pressing them first into the ink on the brush, stabs into the skin.

One day of tattooing consists of 2 or 3 hours of work. The largest area I had done in a single session was maybe 12 cm x 12 cm. Of course how much you can get done in one day depends on your condition. Some days you can go for longer, sometimes shorter. The places that hurt the most are the stomach and the buttocks. On the other hand, the shoulders and arms are relatively easy. The pain is a steady pricking that gradually gets unbearable.

As soon as the session is over I get in the bath. Initially there is an incredible rush of pain, but it eventually subsides and shifts to a dull pain. Then the area starts to swell up and get so fat I can't bend anything. After that my skin usually peels off twice. Interestingly hair continues to grow in the tattooed area.

The Bokashi, or fill work, was all done by the famous Horisan, who is from Osaka. I have the 11th century priest Mongaku doing ascetic training on my chest and stomach, on my back I have Kusunoki Masatsura fighting a demon, on my right arm I have Ume Maru fighting a dragon, on my left arm I have Oniwa fighting a giant murderous carp and on my head a butterfly along with a thrice-coiled snake (see illustrations on the following page.)

I have even participated in the Sakai Festival and I have to say most people gave me a wide berth. Even the police left me alone and didn't scold me. However, anytime I go to the beach I invariably attract a crowd, which can be quite troublesome.

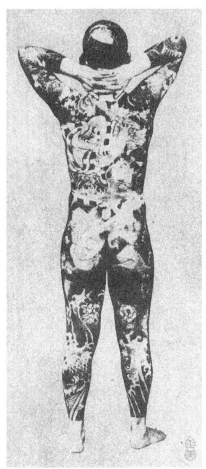
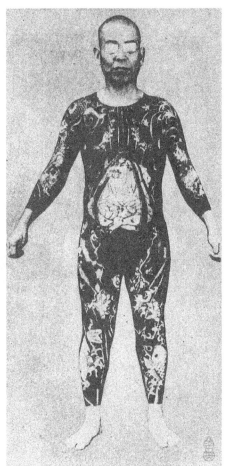

文覚上人 **Mongaku** was an 11th century Shingon priest. After mistakenly killing a Samurai's wife he travelled the country doing Kugyo, painful, ascetic training. This scene shows Mongaku being visited by Lord Fudo while meditating under a waterfall. Edo Era print by Toyoshihara Kunichika.

楠多門丸 **Kusunoki Masatsura** was an early 14th century samurai. In this scene he is fighting a demon. He is considered to be a paragon of loyalty and filial piety. Edo Era Utagawa School print.

梅丸 **Ume Maru** was the illegitimate son of the 14th century warlord Hōjō Takatoki. He is considered to be a model of Samurai bravery. In this scene he is fighting off a dragon. Edo Era Utagawa School print.

西塔鬼若丸 **Saitō Oniwakamaru** is the name the 12th century warrior-monk Benkei had as a child. He is fighting a giant carp that was eating women and children. Edo Era Utagawa School print.

Timeline of Tattooing in Japan	
Date	Historical Occurrence
6th century BCE	The Five Punishments developed in China, one of which is tattooing.
pre-history ~ 300 CE	Chinese envoys make contact with Japan and report tattooing
700 CE~	The first written Japanese histories emerge and discuss tattooing among tribes like the Hayato as well as those working with animals. Tattooing as punishment is mentioned.
700~1587	Few, if any, sources mention tattooing outside references to ascetic religious practices. Tattooing was likely being practiced in Hokkaido, Okinawa and Kyushu.
1587	500 Satsuma (from Kyushu) soldiers discovered with tattoos
1621	Italian Girolamo de Angelis describes tattooed women in Hokkaido.
1624	*A Collection of This and That* contains the line, *It is said that from days long past tattooing was popular primarily with young people.* Suggesting a sub-culture of tattooing was present from before the Edo Era.
1680	The book *Great Mirror of the Erotic* way describes courtesans tattooing themselves with the names of clients
1715	References to the popularity of tattooing, called Iribokuro "Tattooed Moles" amongst gangs of young men.

1720	Tokugawa Yoshimune adds tattooing and beating with a bamboo rod wrapped in cord to the punishments to be administered to criminals.
1720	First record of tattoos being used as punishment in Edo Era Japan
1721	A line from *The Woman-Killer and the Hell of Oil* reads, *Men that work as collectors will often have all manner of things tattooed on their bodies. To end arguments they will make as if reaching into their Kimono thereby revealing the markings.*
1764	Bakin talks about the state of tattooing, *When I was still sporting a child's haircut (1764-1781) the gamblers and ruffians I saw were covered with tattoos. I'm sure that tattooing was common even before that.*
1766	Ueda Akinaru in *All Manner of Tales from a Wise Monkey,* *In Edo the various gangs of Otokodate are always competing with each other. They will have their entire arms festooned with Iribokuro "tattooed moles" or even have their whole torsos covered with dragons. Sometimes on their back you will see the severed head of Mikenjaku.*
1779	Captain James Cook made three voyages to the South Pacific 1766-1779. When Cook and his men returned home to Europe from their voyages to Polynesia, they told tales of the 'tattooed savages' they had seen using the word "tattoo" derived from the Tahitian *Tatau.*

1782	Definition of 刺字 Shiji differentiates between Irezumi and Horimono. *Criminals arrested for the first or second time for robbing or stealing will be tattooed with the two lines on the upper arm. For people caught embezzling funds this punishment will be relaxed....What these people have is called Irezumi. On the other hand, people that used a needle to stab the shape of a dragon in blue all over their body like Nine Dragons from Water Margin call that Horimono.*
1800	Mishima Kanuemon describes the condition of 160 people banished to Hachijo Island. *They have tattooing on their arms and shoulders with no gap between. For example dragons, tigers, plums, bamboo and large letters engraved in. You can also see severed head of women with a scroll in her mouth.*
1808	Publication of an edition of Water Margin illustrated by Utagawa Kuniyoshi
1810	Publication of *The Tattooed Arm* by Shikite Sanba and Utakuni Kunimitsu.
1811	Tokugawa Government issues 1st prohibition on tattooing
1842	Tokugawa Government issues 2nd prohibition on tattooing
1868	End of the Edo Era beginning of the Meiji Era ~1912
1872	Government issues 3rd prohibition on tattooing

1883	The German Dr. Baltz estimates there are 30,000 tattooed people in Tokyo in his Journal.
1888	Hokkaido Ainu tattoo survey by Hirai Masagoro
1894	Sasamori Gisuke's *Exploration of the Southern Islands* recorded the meanings behind Ryukyu tattoos.
1899	Tattooing banned in Okinawa
1934	In *Footsteps of the Ainu* Michioka Shinichi discusses tattooing method.

End

Tattoos as Punishment
An Illustrated History of Japanese Tattooing
Volume One

Bibliography

田中香涯 (1874-1944) 醫事雑考: 妖。異。變 1941	小野友道 戦国時代のいれずみ 2008
Early Chinese Tattoo Carrie E. Reed. Sino-Platonic Papers #103 June 2000	Kono Isamu (1901 – 1967) *A Critique of Facial Tattooing on Clay Figurines* 1932
鳥居竜蔵 1870-1953 北千島アイヌの入墨 1903 有史以前乃日本 1918	植木直一郎 1878-1959 現代語訳古事記 1943
坪井正五郎 アイヌの婦人 1889 アイヌの入れ墨 1893	松田修 刺青・性・死 1972 日本刺青論　松田修 1989
満岡伸一, 1882-1950 アイヌの足跡 1934	安田徳太郎 日本のイレズミ風俗 1952
神宮司庁 1908-1930 古事類苑第 20 冊	藤田新太郎 徳川幕府刑事図譜 1893.
玉林晴朗 1898-1945 文身百姿 1936	使鰕夷行記　江戸
江馬務 剳青の史的研究 1923 入墨 1934 入墨経験談 1934	松野正彦 十勝アイヌ文身の研究 北大解剖研究報告 第 113 号、1958 年 11 月
八木奘三郎 日本考古学 *1902*	笹森儀助 南島探験 1894
大野延太郎 1863-1938 土中の文化:考古学研究資料 1931	寺田精一 文身研究の興味 1912 文身の話 1912
Mimori Sadao *Primitive Cultures of Japan* 1931	WWWJDIC: Online Japanese Dictionary Service
田中祐吉, 1874-1944 変態風俗の研究 1927	nihonshinwa.com

CPSIA information can be obtained
at www.ICGtesting.com
Printed in the USA
LVHW041039100423
743960LV00014B/443